VOICE *for* LIFE

SONGBOOK

RS✦M

IMPORTANT NOTICE: PLEASE READ THIS BEFORE MAKING ANY COPIES.

We have provided both full score, with piano accompaniment and choral parts for all the songs in this book.
You MAY NOT PHOTOCOPY the full piano score.
You may make copies of the choral parts FOR LOCAL USE ONLY.
Under no circumstances may copies be sold – even to members of your choir.

Please include every item that you copy in your annual CCLI report, quoting the 'Voice for Life Songbook'.
This doesn't cost you, your church or school anything but it does ensure that composers and authors get due
financial recognition for their work. It also enables the RSCM to train the church musicians of tomorrow.

We have made every effort to identify all copyright holders and to all of them we are most grateful.
We apologise if there are errors or omissions and we will correct them in future printings.

Permission to perform the works in this collection in public (except in the course of divine worship) should
normally be obtained from the Performing Right Society Ltd, 29/33 Berners Street, London W1P 4AA
or its affiliated Societies in each country throughout the world, unless the owner or the occupier of the premises
being used holds a licence from the Society. Permission to make a recording of the works must be obtained in
advance from the Mechanical-Copyright Protection Society Ltd, Elgar House, 41 Streatham High Road, London
SW16 1ER, or its affiliated Societies in each country throughout the world.

ISBN: 0854021108
Order Number: F0110
Compiled and edited by Esther Jones and Leah Perona-Wright
Cover design by Anthony Marks
Typesetting by Leah Perona-Wright
Music editing by David Iliff
Printed in Great Britain by Halstan & Co.

The following copyright owners are members of CCLI. If your church owns a CCLI Music Reproduction Licence
or School Collective Worship Music Reproduction Licence, you may copy the choral parts of their items, FOR LOCAL
USE ONLY, without further permission. You are requested, however, to report all items you copy on your yearly
CCLI returns. If you don't hold either a CCL or CWMRL licence, please contact the copyright holders directly.

Maranatha! Music and Hope Publishing Company
both administered by CopyCare, PO Box 77, Hailsham, East Sussex BN27 3EF
Phone: 01323 840942 email: music@copycare.com

Wild Goose Publications, Copyright Department, Fourth Floor, Savoy House, 140 Sauchiehall Street,
Glasgow G2 3DH, Scotland. Phone: 0141 332 6292

To purchase a CCLI Music Reproduction Licence, please contact:
CCL Ltd. P.O. Box 1339, Eastbourne, East Sussex BN21 4YF,
Phone: 01323 417711 email: sales@ccli.co.uk

The following publishers have granted permission to copy the chorus parts only for FOR LOCAL USE ONLY
without further permission or licence. For other usage, please contact the Copyright Department at
The Royal School of Church Music.

Oxford University Press, Great Clarendon Street, Oxford OX2 6DP
Faber Music Limited, 3 Queen Square, London WC1N 3AU
The Royal School of Church Music, 19 The Close, Salisbury, Wiltshire SP1 2EB
Church of Scotland Panel on Worship, 121 George Street, Edinburgh EH2 4YN
Christian Conference of Asia, 96 Pak Tin Village Area 2, Mei Tin Road, Shatin NT, Hong Kong SAR, CHINA

Preface

It's vitally important, if you want to engage the singers in a choir, to choose the right repertoire. When working with young people or inexperienced adults, it can be difficult to find music of a suitable standard which combines integrity and artistic merit. The *Voice for Life Songbook* is designed to solve this problem. It offers choir trainers a wealth of music which will inspire and enthuse singers of all ages, starting with songs suitable for those who are new to singing, and moving on to pieces designed to offer a gentle challenge as people grow in confidence and skill.

This anthology is part of the *Voice for Life* initiative, through which the Royal School of Church Music aims to encourage and enable high standards in choral education and singing. The backbone of *Voice for Life* is a training programme for singers delivered by their choir trainer within the choral context. Thousands of choristers around the world are already benefiting from *Voice for Life* and, with numbers rapidly increasing, the RSCM is working on a number of educational resources to support them and supplement the core textbook, *The Choir Trainer's Book*.

The *Voice for Life Songbook*, produced by experienced choir trainers, music teachers and singers, is the first song collection published as part of the scheme. In line with the aims of *Voice for Life,* it offers guidance to the choir trainer on running rehearsals, teaching repertoire and developing the vocal and musical skills of singers. And through it, the RSCM hopes to fulfil its mission to enrich the present, secure the future and sustain the traditions.

I would happily recommend any music which encourages people to develop that God-given gift, the joy of singing – and the *Voice for Life Songbook* is an ideal place to start.

Brian Kay

Brian Kay
RSCM Vice-President

Contents

Contents

Rehearsals

It is important to rehearse regularly to maintain the motivation and commitment of your singers. As a general rule, it is good to rehearse weekly although you may need extra rehearsals when leading up to a special concert or service.

Long and badly planned rehearsals are often counter-productive and result in singers of any age feeling bored and frustrated. From the very start, balance your rehearsal time so that you include time for warm-ups, vocal training and learning repertory. By building in a variety of tasks you will keep your singers concentration and interest.

Tips on rehearsing and improving your choir:

- Make sure that everyone can see you, and that they have room to see and move. Two or three rows of singers in a slight arc should provide the most successful layout.

- Your choir will need to stand to sing for some if not all of the rehearsal. When sitting to sing, make sure that children are seated on chairs or benches and not on the floor, as this will restrict their stomach muscles.

- Try and rehearse your choir in the largest space available to you so that your singers can be encouraged to project their voices. When leading up to a performance, where possible, try and arrange a rehearsal where the performance will take place so that your singers are prepared for the acoustic and layout.

- Make sure your rehearsal room is well ventilated so that it is not too stuffy, otherwise singers will become lethargic and find it hard to concentrate. Equally a rehearsal room that is cold will all too often cause singers instinctively to raise their shoulders to keep warm – this causes tension in the throat and jaw and also limits the blood supply to the heart which makes you colder.

- When you have a long rehearsal, make sure that singers are given a break, perhaps building in a rhythm game or similar, so that your singers are able to rest their voices for a few minutes, and regain their concentration. You may like to encourage them to bring water and some food to keep their energy levels up.

- Unless you have perfect pitch, the use of a piano, keyboard or other instrument is essential to help you pitch the starting notes of songs accurately. Singing with an accompaniment can be a real motivating factor for singers, when they can hear how their vocal part fits with the rest of the music.

- Where possible see if you can find an accompanist for your rehearsals. This will allow you to concentrate entirely on the singing. It may also mean that you can split the choir into groups and run sectional rehearsals working on individual parts.

- When singing unaccompanied, practise pitching the first note quietly and accurately.

- Teach everything by demonstrating as well as you can. This means that you must know the music well yourself, and have developed your own singing as much as you can. Where possible, always demonstrate by singing, rather than by playing the piano, as you want to provide your singers with a vocal sound to copy.

- Look and listen as your choir sings, and avoid singing along with them. Try to analyse where there are problems, and how they might be put right. Tackle one problem at a time.

- Always be positive, even when you are correcting faults.

- Make sure you know the music well enough so you can look around at your singers while you are conducting. It is important to have eye contact with your singers while they perform. Wait until everyone is watching you before you start a piece. While performing a piece, see if you can get eye contact with every member of the choir.

- Do not single out the less able singers in front of the other singers and do not let anyone make rude comments about their singing.

- Never ask a poor singer to stop singing or stand at the back. Place a weak singer with two better singers, one on either side, without making it obvious why you are doing it.

- Begin your rehearsals with warm-ups, targeting areas you think may need improving. Try and incorporate difficult phrases from the pieces you are learning so that the warm-ups prepare them for the work later in the rehearsal.

- When working with children, you will find it easier to encourage them to perform with confidence if they have memorized the words and music. Particularly at primary school level, it is often unnecessary to use printed words or music at all. If you do need music/words for any of the songs, you may find an overhead projector useful. This enables children to look forward as they sing, rather than looking down at word sheets.

- A greater sense of involvement, performance and enjoyment can be achieved if the choir is encouraged to move as it sings. If you include actions or movement, remember to practise these individually; the visual effect should enhance the performance without distracting singers from musical accuracy.

- Always end the rehearsal with a 'performance' of a piece, or part of a piece, which the choir can sing well. This will send them away with a sense of achievement.

- Encourage your singers to sing at home, so they are not just singing just once or twice a week, but daily. Singing is no different from playing an instrument – the more regularly you sing, the better you become.

There is more extensive advice available on the practicalities of running a choir in the *Voice for Life Choir Trainer's Book*.

Warm-ups

It is advisable to begin every rehearsal with a warm-up. The chief purposes of this process, in the words of voice specialists Brenda Smith and Robert T Salatoff, are namely:

1) to adjust the voice from speaking to singing

2) to align the body and free the breathing mechanism for the act of singing

3) to create a physical awareness of the vocal mechanism being used correctly

4) to stretch gently and exercise the skeletal muscles used in phonation

As singers often arrive at a rehearsal from other activities with their minds on other things, the warm-up also helps focus their thoughts and channel their energies ready for the rehearsal.

Structuring a warm-up

A warm-up usually consists of a series of short physical, mental and vocal activities. When planning a session it is helpful to follow the pattern below:

1)   Relaxation

2)   Posture

3)   Breathing

4)   Tone and resonance

5)   Range and flexibility

The exercises listed below are intended as an introductory guide. There are many books that give more detailed advice as well as additional examples of warm-up activities. Many choir trainers will develop their own exercises: it is good to take an imaginative and varied approach to the warming up process in order to keep singers interested and stimulated.

Relaxation

Healthy singing requires a balance between physical relaxation and activity. Many different muscle groups are engaged in the act of singing, but any tension in the body has a detrimental effect on the voice. To release any tension in the body, start with gentle stretches and sighing. If appropriate you could ask choir members to massage each other's shoulders. Other suggestions are listed below.

- Stretch up with one hand, then the other, as if trying to pick apples from the branch of a high tree.

- Starting from a standing position, slowly bend from the waist until you are doubled over. Allow your head and hands to hang loosely. Keep the knees slightly bent and sway from side to side. Take several deep breaths in, and sigh out before slowly standing up.

- Tread on the spot with toes remaining on the ground to loosen ankles and knees.

- Tense every part of the body, starting with the toes and moving up to the face; hold for ten seconds, then release.

- Place the hands on your hips and keep them still as you twist from the torso to the right and left. Hold for seven seconds in each direction.

- Roll shoulders one way then the other to reduce tension. When rolling forward imagine you are trying to make your shoulders touch in front of you. At the back bring your shoulder blades as close as possible.

- Massage your face; then allow the jaw to drop open as if on a hinge.

- Open the mouth and eyes as wide as you can; then screw your face up as tightly as possible. Repeat several times, increasing the speed at which you move between the two.

- Stick out your tongue and move it up, down, side-to-side and in circles. Use it to probe the inside of the mouth, as if moving a sticky sweet from your back teeth.

- Chew imaginary gum in an exaggerated way, trying to engage your whole face in the action.

- Shake your hands as fast as possible, as though you have a piece of sticky tape stuck to them that you want to get off. Shake out your legs as well and then move into position ready to sing.

Posture

The warm-up is an excellent opportunity to reiterate the importance of good posture when singing. (Choir trainers should keep an eye on the posture of their singers throughout the rehearsal as they may need further reminders: as singers tire, tension can creep in and some may start to droop.)

When standing, your singers should have:

1)   Their feet slightly apart and firmly on the ground

2)   Their weight distributed evenly on both feet

3)   A 'tall' posture – with a straight back and the head upright

4)   Relaxed shoulders

5)   Relaxed knees (they should not be locked)

The following activities may help to encourage good posture:

- Stretch up to the ceiling with both hands. Keeping your arms straight, bring them slowly down to your sides as you sigh out. Imagine the back lengthening and widening as you do this and don't allow your chest to collapse. As you sing try to retain a sense of space and release around your ribs.

- Mime tying a piece of string to the crown of your head and imagine gently pulling it up towards the ceiling. Add more pieces of thread to fix the top of your chest to the ceiling and your shoulders diagonally to the corners of the room.

- Imagine your head is a helium balloon floating on top of your body. Allow it to move freely in figure of eight patterns.

Breathing

When practising breathing, it is easy for the body to become tense. You need to check that your singers stay relaxed while you practise breathing exercises with them. In particular look for the following:

1)   The shoulders should not move when breathing in or out

2)   The chest should not move upwards when breathing in

3)   Inhalation, whether through the mouth or nose, should remain silent. Any noise at the intake of breath indicates tension in the body.

Here are some exercises to practise breathing:

- Breathe out; then, when you reach the end of the stream of air, release to allow the air to rush back into your lungs through your mouth. Feel how the air is cool against the roof and back of your mouth. Hold your breath for a few seconds and then sigh out. Repeat the exercise with your hands round your waist to feel how it expands as you breathe in and contracts as you exhale.

- Place your right hand on your left shoulder and take a deep breath. You should find that this causes you to breathe low in your body rather than taking a shallow breath at the top of your chest – which is what you should aim for every time you breathe to sing. Repeat with your left hand on your right shoulder.

- Pant gently for a few seconds as if you are a dog trying to cool off. (Don't try this exercise for too long otherwise you will find it makes you dizzy!)

- Hold up one finger at arm's length from your face. Imagine it is a candle that needs to be blown out. Take a deep breath and blow energetically. Repeat the exercise, increasing the number of fingers you are holding up and blowing out each in turn.

- Breathe in silently over four counts, then let the air escape to a steady 'shh' over another four counts. Instead of holding your breath in between the inhalation and the exhalation, try to imagine it is a smooth, circular process. Repeat the exercise a few times, then try the same thing on a 'zzz' or 'vvv' sound at a comfortable pitch. Gradually build up to eight, twelve and sixteen counts.

Tone and resonance

When you start to engage the voice in the warm-up process, it is best to start with humming, gentle slides or short patterns of notes in a narrow range. Start in the middle of the register and move downwards first to exercise the lower vocal range before gradually extending it upwards. You should try to include both legato and staccato sounds. The following exercises can be used in this process:

- Sing the word 'sing' and sustain the 'ng' sound at the end. Feel how it makes your nose and lips vibrate. This is called an open-mouthed hum. Slide up a major third and then down again. Repeat the exercise moving down a semitone each time.

- On a rolled 'r' or lip trill, slide around in the lower to upper middle range of your voice. Mirror the movement with your hands as you ascend and descend in pitch.

- Try a series of exaggerated yawns, starting higher with each yawn and sliding down to the bottom of your voice on an 'ah' sound. You might like to stretch each time you yawn.

- Make low, resonant 'vvv' and 'zzz' sounds. Feel the vibrations that these sounds produce around your lips and teeth. Starting in the middle of your range sing a descending triad on 'va' sound, keeping the 'v' as active and resonant as possible. Repeat the exercise, moving down in semitones.

- Sing the same note five times on an 'oo' vowel. Make the first four short and detached and the last sustained. Repeat the exercise a semitone higher each time and introduce other vowels, e.g. ee, aw, ah, eh.

- On a vowel of your choice, slide up a fifth and back down again. Repeat the exercise moving a semitone higher each time. When your singers are comfortable with this you can increase the interval of the slide to an octave.

- Using a bright 'ya' sound, sing a five-note descending scale. Repeat starting a semitone higher each time.

Range and flexibility

After some initial vocal exercises you can move on to activities that require greater stamina and agility. These can include scales and arpeggios of an octave range or more, and exercises with fast semiquaver runs or long phrases that demand good breath control.

You could also try using tongue-twisters with your singers. Using one of the following examples, or making up your own, ask your singers to sing a simple melodic pattern such as a descending scale, with the tongue twister on each note of the scale:

● 'Red lorry, yellow lorry'

● 'Gin and tonic'

● 'Merry men'

At this stage in the warm-up you may also like to include a short warm-up song or canon (examples of which can be found in this anthology). Songs with actions are particularly helpful as they get the singers moving.

Additional warm-up activities that relate to the songs in this book can be found in the 'Preparation' section of the training notes that accompany each piece. While these relate to specific aspects of each song they may also be used as part of a general warm up.

More extensive guidance on warming up and exercising the voice may be found in the *Voice for Life Choir Trainer's Book*.

How to use the *Voice for Life Songbook*

The *Voice for Life Songbook* has been compiled in line with the *Voice for Life* philosophy, to give singers the opportunity to:

- enjoy using their voices
- learn to use their voices well
- experience a range of musical styles
- sing both accompanied and a cappella
- develop their musical skills and understanding

The Songbook contains a range of material compiled with young people and singers at beginner and intermediate levels in mind. With traditional church music, gospel and jazz, and songs from around the world, this volume will appeal to singers of all ages, and provide your choir with the opportunity to explore a range of musical styles.

The majority of songs in this collection can be sung by everyone, and are designed to help you develop the confidence of your singers as you progress through the book:

Warm-up songs, rounds and canons
These are short songs which are ideal for use at the start of a rehearsal as part of a warm-up. Some are 'call and response' songs, others are short action songs or rounds which include optional ostinato parts. You will find that most of these songs can be taught by rote without using the music.

Unison songs
A selection of songs for unison voices, some of which are written in a simple verse-chorus structure, and others are more developed.

Unison with descant
The majority of songs in this section have been designed to be flexible, so the descant is often optional, depending on the capability of your choir and the resources available to you.

Two parts and more
The songs in this section range from short songs with ostinato accompaniment to help develop part-singing (up to four parts), to longer songs and anthems.

The vocal parts in this Songbook are photocopiable so you can provide the singers in your choir with the music. (This permission to photocopy applies only to the purchaser's own choir or group. Any pages which may be photocopied are clearly marked 'You may photocopy this page' at the bottom of the revelant pages). Do not feel that your singers must always use the music though: they will have a far greater freedom of movement, will have a greater sense of ensemble and will be able to watch you conducting more closely if they can also learn to sing from memory.

A demonstration of each song is included on the accompanying CD. This is intended for those who would like guidance on how a particular song should sound, and also for those who are not confident at reading music, so they can listen to their part and learn it. There is an additional CD available from RSCM Music Direct which contains piano accompaniments of each song in the book for you to use in rehearsals if you do not have a pianist.

The training notes which accompany each piece provide ideas about how you might introduce the song to your singers in rehearsals, ideas for a creative performance, and how you can use the song to develop your singers' voices and musical understanding. Less experienced choir trainers may like to follow the training notes in detail, whereas those who are more experienced may prefer to simply dip into the notes for ideas.

To help you in the task of developing your singers' voices as well as their musical skills and understanding, the *Voice for Life Singer's Workbooks* and *Choir Trainer's Book* are a useful backup resource. These contain a variety of teaching aids such as theory games and exercises, photocopiable worksheets, vocal exercises, and plenty of guidance about how to introduce each new concept or idea to your singers as well as practical advice on running your choir.

We hope you enjoy singing the repertoire in this book as you rehearse, perform and develop your singers' confidence and musical skills.

Esther Jones
Co-Director of *Voice for Life*

Leah Perona-Wright
Co-Director of *Voice for Life*

Warm-up songs, rounds and canons

1. Amen, say Amen

⦿ Track 1

Information

This call and response song by Ken Burton is in a jazz/blues style and is loosely based on the twelve-bar blues chord pattern. It is an action song which allows singers to engage the body as well as the voice and its limited vocal range makes it an ideal warm-up song. Its structure allows different members of the group to take it in turns to be the leader and can also be used as a basis for improvisation.

Teaching the song

This song is catchy and memorable and is best learnt without reading from the score. You can introduce actions from the start (e.g. clap/stamp): you should make them rhythmical but remember that they don't have to copy the rhythm of the melody.

Teach the first four bars by singing each phrase of the melody and asking your singers to sing it back to you as an echo. In the first bar on the word 'hands' slide up the semitone from the grace note to the harmony note, in keeping with the musical style. Teach the last three bars separately as the call and response pattern changes here. Make sure that everyone can hear the difference between the A flats and A naturals so that they are in tune. Also, make sure the response stays in time – if your singers wait for the leader to finish singing before taking a breath it is liable to become late.

Go through the whole song several times until it is secure. Introduce a new action each time (e.g. stamp your feet, wave your hands, slap your knees, praise the Lord): encourage singers to use their imagination here.

Be creative

Once the song is well-known ask other choir members take it in turns to be the leader. If you sing it standing in a circle the role of the leader can pass all the way round so that no one misses out. As they become more confident they may want to improvise their own melodies: encourage them to experiment and take risks and praise them for doing so. Make sure that the choir always copies them exactly: it is excellent ear training!

Musical skills and understanding

'Call and response' is a pattern of alternation between the voice of an individual and the voice of the congregation, as occurs in this song. It allows individual sorrows, hopes, and joys to be shared by the community.

One of the characteristics of this style of music is the inclusion of 'blue notes'. These are chromatic notes that are foreign to the key the piece is in. Ask the singers to try to identify the key (F major); then find the blue notes (e.g. G sharp in bar 1 and A flat in bar 3 of the voice part – some may be able to identify that these are the same note on the piano even though they have different names).

Encourage singers to listen to the piano part, which contains some bluesy chords. Explain that the quaver movement in the left hand of the piano part is known as a walking bass line – it was popular with Bach as well as jazz musicians!

1. Amen, say Amen

Music: Ken Burton

* the group leader can choose any action
† the group sings and does the action

2. Hallelu, hallelu

Information

This joyful song from the gospel tradition encourages us to rejoice and praise God. Although we think of it being an English word, 'Hallelujah' is originally Hebrew and literally means 'praise Yahweh' (God). When sung with actions (see below) this song is good for warming up as it requires singers to engage their minds and bodies as well as their voices.

Teaching the song

This song is from the oral tradition and is best learnt in a call and response pattern without reading from the score. Teach it in four-bar phrases by singing the melody and asking your singers to sing it back to you as an echo. Take particular care over bars with the syncopated rhythm (bars 7, 9, 11, 13 and 15) to ensure it is together. If it proves problematic you might try externalising the rhythm by asking the singers to clap it or make up an action to fit it. Sing through the whole song several times until it is secure.

Be creative

Once the song is well-known divide your singers into two teams and ask them to sit down. Ask the first team to sing all the 'Hallelujahs' and the other all the 'Praise ye the Lords'. Tell them that they should only stand up while they sing. This is not too difficult in the first half of the song, but they will have to be fairly agile in the second half as the phrases are shorter!

If you want to repeat the song you can make the piano introduction an interlude between the repeats. You could encourage your singers to improvise their own riffs on scat syllables (e.g., doo-wop, shoo-be-do etc.) over the chord patterns – it may help to keep playing the same chords on a loop while they experiment (G2, C6/G, G2, C6/G). More experienced singers may be able to harmonize each others' melodies to enable the piece to take on a life of its own.

Musical skills and understanding

One of the features of this arrangement is the syncopated rhythm of 'Praise ye the Lord'. Explain that syncopated rhythms put emphasis on the off-beats rather than the main beats of the bar. They are very common in pop music and jazz. Ask them to identify syncopated rhythms in other pieces of music, or make up their own.

2. Hallelu, hallelu

Music: Traditional
arranged by Esther Jones

3. Kyrie eleison

⊙   **Track 3**

Information

The source of this short canon is unknown. Its traditional words are 'Ah, poor bird/Take thy flight/Far above the sorrows of this dark night' but, set to the 'Kyrie eleison' text (which is Greek, meaning 'Lord, have mercy') it can be used as a prayer response.

Teaching the song

When rehearsing this song insist that the choir sing as legato as possible. To achieve this, start by singing the melody on a single vowel, e.g. 'ah' or 'oo'. Encourage them to slide between the notes to connect them up. Once these connections are established, ask them to make the slides imperceptible to the listener. Next you could try singing the melody with the text, but miss out the consonants. Lastly, add in the words, making the vowels as long as possible and not allowing the consonants to get in the way of the flow. If you are not sure of the pronunciation of the Greek, listen to the demonstration on the CD.

Ask your singers to sing two bars to a breath. To encourage them to control the flow of the breath, suggest that they draw an arc in the air as they sing each phrase. Tell them that they need to control the time and speed of the arc so it coincides exactly with the phrase they are singing. Those running out of breath too quickly will find that they arrive at the end of their arc too soon.

Be creative

This song can be sung in unison, two-part canon (with entries at Figure 1 and Figure 3) or in four parts. It can be sung a cappella or with piano accompaniment and flute. Try to be imaginative when you think about how to perform it. You could even end with a quiet, hummed verse to create a sense of atmosphere. As there are no dynamics marked you will have to make your own decisions about how loud or soft you want each repetition.

Musical skills and understanding

There is another traditional canon that shares this melody but it is in the major key rather than the minor. Can anyone work out which notes would need to change in order for it to be sung in C major rather than C minor? Try singing it. Does it still suit the 'Kyrie eleison' text?

3. Kyrie eleison

Music: Traditional
arranged Esther Jones

VOICE

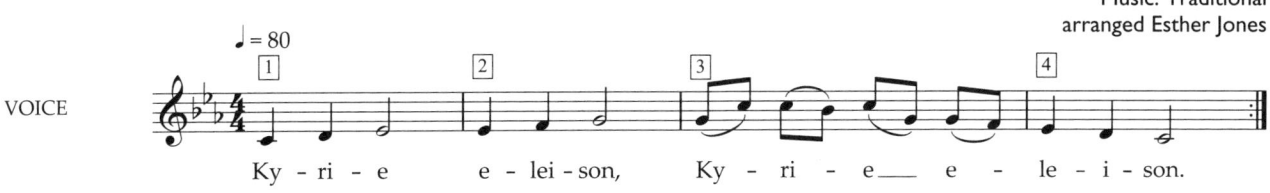

Ky – ri – e   e – lei – son,   Ky – ri – e ___ e – le – i – son.

PIANO
OSTINATO

FLUTE/RECORDER
OSTINATO

4. When the Spirit of the Lord

⊙ **Track 4**

Information

This song is in a traditional Jewish klezmer style. It refers to David, a Jewish King from the Old Testament who was a musician and probably wrote some of the songs in the book of Psalms. The Bible records (in 2 Samuel) that David once praised God by dancing wearing only a linen ephod – the equivalent of his underwear! In the last verse of this song, as the music gets faster and more frenzied, you can imagine David losing his inhibitions and dancing before the Lord with all his might.

Preparation

Ask your singers what key the music is in. Have they noticed that even though it shares a key signature with G major, it is actually in E minor? The big clues are the D sharps throughout the piece and that it starts and ends on an E minor chord. Try singing an E minor scale before you begin the piece. More advanced singers may know the difference between a harmonic and melodic minor scale. Can they sing them both?

Teaching the song

This song can easily be taught without the music, in four-bar phrases. Learn it in unison first then, if appropriate, try adding the lower part at bar 11. It follows the same pattern as the melodic line but is a third lower throughout (the only exception being the last two notes). Don't forget that when you perform the song you should start slowly and get faster with each successive verse – experiment to see how fast you can sing at the end of the song without losing the ensemble.

Be creative

In verse 2 you may like to clap a rhythm in bars 6, 10, 14 and 18 to illustrate the words. Ask your singers to suggest something suitable.

Can they think of actions for any of the other verses? (You will need to consider how easily these actions can be performed while singing, before asking the whole choir to do them!).

Using the voice well

See if your singers can sing each four-bar phrase in a single breath. Every time they fill up with air they should think about keeping the breath low in their body, rather than taking a shallow gasp. Remind them that their shoulders should not move as they take a breath and that their body needs to stay poised but relaxed during the process.

Musical skills and understanding

Ask your singers to identify the lowest and highest notes that they sing in this piece. Do they know the names of the pitches?

Check that your singers know the Italian term for 'get faster' (*accelerando*).

4. When the Spirit of the Lord

Music: Traditional
arranged Esther Jones

Slowly at first, then with increasing pace

2. When the Spirit of the Lord is within my heart,
   I will clap as David clapped . . . .

3. When the Spirit of the Lord is within my heart,
   I will dance as David danced . . . .

4. When the Spirit of the Lord is within my heart,
   I will praise as David praised . . . .

5. King of kings

Information

This canon is an ancient Hebrew folk song. The text by Sophie Conty and Naomi Batya draws on names given to Jesus in the Bible. 'King of kings' and 'Lord of lords' are used in the book of Revelation when John sees Jesus appear as a rider on a white horse. 'Prince of Peace' is the name used by the Old Testament prophet Isaiah.

Teaching the song

This song can easily be taught by rote in two-bar phrases. Put in the claps as marked from the start to help your singers learn the rhythm. Once it is very familiar you can try it as a two-part round.

In order to be able to follow the tempo direction and get faster each time you sing it, you will need to take care that both parts speed up by the same amount. To do this, singers will need to watch the conductor and listen carefully to the other part. Young singers might be tempted to put their hands over their ears so they don't get put off by people singing the other part; but if they can't hear everyone else they are liable to sing out of time and the ensemble will be lost.

Be creative

You may like to teach your singers the ostinato parts to accompany the song. Be creative when you plan how to perform the song and ask your singers to suggest how you fit the parts together – you could, for example, build up the ostinato parts one at a time and then add the melody; alternatively, you could sing through the melody with the piano and then add the ostinato parts. If the melody and piano parts drop out towards the end you could try fading out as often happens at the end of pop songs, by getting quieter until the audience is straining to hear.

Using the voice well

Can the singers on the ostinato parts manage the whole phrase in a single breath? The last bar of each ostinato part needs to be sung very legato: make sure singers don't aspirate between the notes, putting in a small 'h' sound as they change pitch. To iron this out ask them to practice sliding between the notes. Then speed up the slide so it is imperceptible to the listener but so that the notes stay connected. Singers should always aim to connect up the notes in this way when singing legato.

Musical skills and understanding

An ostinato is a short melody or pattern that is constantly repeated, usually in the same part at the same pitch. Can anyone think of any other pieces that use ostinatos?

Ask your singers if they think this song is written in a major or minor key. Discuss how they came to their decision. (Singers often describe major keys as sounding 'happy' and therefore may find it difficult to identify *King of kings* as minor because it builds up to a fast tempo and has positive lyrics such as 'Glory, hallelujah'. If they have trouble understanding, why not sing this song in a major key so they can hear and experience the difference!)

5. King of kings

Words: Sophie Conty and Naomi Batya

Music: Hebrew folksong
arranged Esther Jones

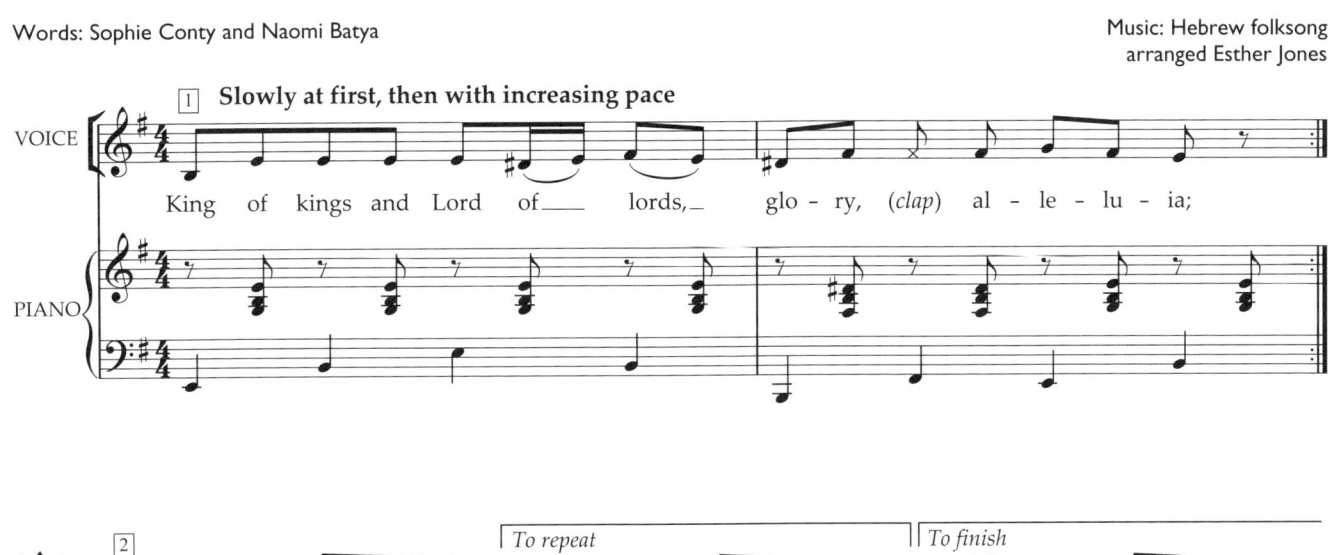

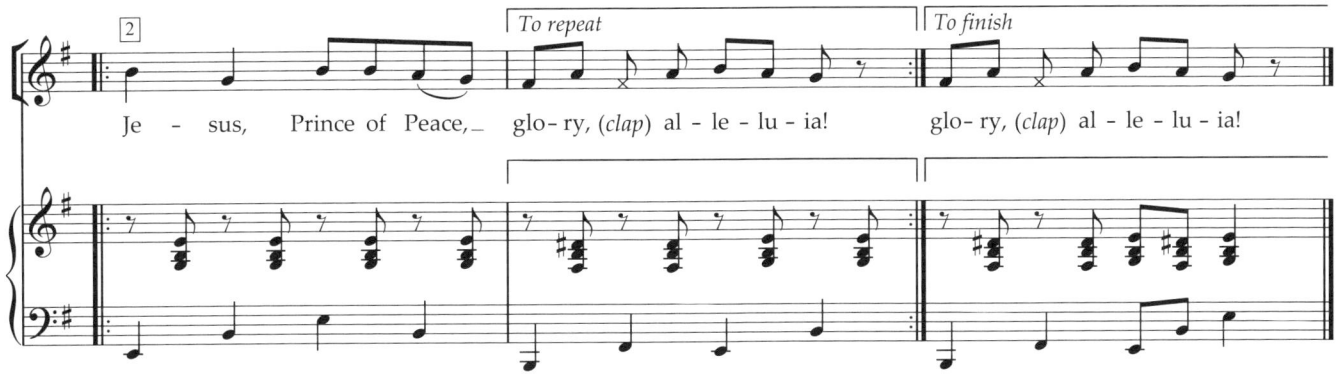

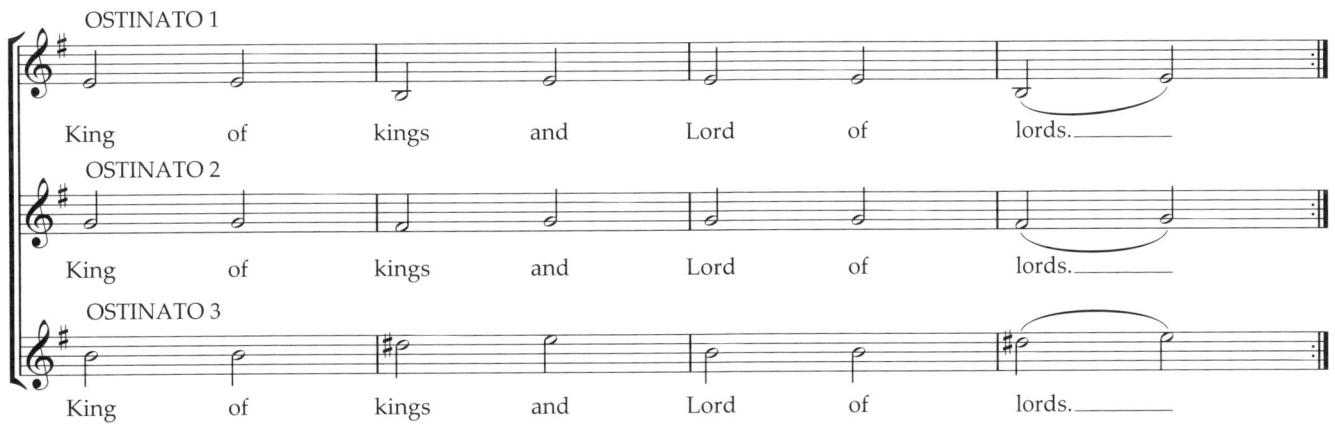

6. Shalom chaverim

 Track 6

Information

The Hebrew word 'Shalom' is used on a daily basis in Israel to greet people or bid them farewell: it is also understood around the world to mean 'peace'. 'Shalom' (Prince of Peace) is one of the descriptive names the Bible uses to indicate the ministry and personality of the Messiah.

The words of this song transalated into English are: 'Shalom, my friends, shalom, my friends, shalom, shalom; Till we meet again, till we meet again, shalom, shalom.'

'Lehitraot' is literally 'until seeing each other [again]' as in 'Auf wiedersehen' (German) or 'Au revoir' (French).

Teaching the song

Ask your singers to greet each other with the words 'Shalom chaverim'. They should pronounce 'ch' as in the Scottish 'loch' and 'im' as 'eem'.

This song is from the oral tradition and can be taught without the music in two-bar phrases. Once it is familiar, encourage your singers to sing four bars to one breath.

When it is secure, try singing it as a two-part round, with the second part coming in when the first part reaches figure 3. Once this can be sung with confidence, try it in four parts.

Using the voice well

The first note of the piece is quite low for most singers and may therefore sound a little weaker than the rest of the phrase. Encourage your singers to find a full, resonant sound for this note so that it can be heard.

Some singers may find it difficult to sing legato in bars 5–6. To help them achieve this, suggest that they make the vowels as long as possible, particularly on the 'hit' of 'lehitraot'. You could also practice this phrase without the consonants, sliding between the notes to make it as smooth as possible – but make sure it stays legato when you reintroduce the consonants.

Musical skills and understanding

At a first glance this song appears to be in E minor but it is missing the characteristic D sharp that is usually found in this key. This is because it is written in the Aeolian mode (also known as the natural minor) – a scale used in folk music around the world. You may like to ask your singers to sing this scale before they rehearse the piece. Can they identify the pattern of tones and semitones?

You can also play the Aeolian mode on the piano starting on A and then playing all the white notes up to the next A.

6. Shalom chaverim

Peace, friends!

Music: Hebrew folksong
arranged Geoff Weaver

7. Rejoice in the Lord always

Information

This short two-part canon is simple enough to teach to the congregation in a church service, school assembly or at a concert. The text is from Paul's letter to the Philippians 4:4.

Teaching the song

Teach this song in a call and response pattern in four-bar phrases. There's no need for the singers to use the music. From the start encourage your singers to sing four bars in one breath by demonstrating this yourself. Once the song is secure, try singing it as a two-part canon.

Using the voice well

The word 'rejoice' contains a diphthong – a combination of two vowels in the same syllable. In order for the choir to be unanimous when singing this word, they will need to change vowel at the same time. Singers usually leave the change of vowel as late as possible. In this instance it means hanging onto the 'aw' sound in 'rejoice' and then changing onto the 'ee' sound just before the 'ce' sound needs to arrive. Practice this slowly and gradually increase the speed as it becomes easier.

Singers may be tempted to slide between the first two notes of bars 9 and 10, 13 and 14. While the notes need to be connected in order to achieve a legato sound, the movement between them should be imperceptible.

Musical skills and understanding

The melody of this song mostly moves in step (tones and semitones) but there are a few bigger leaps. Can the singers identify where these occur and can they name the intervals (e.g. a perfect fourth between the first two notes)?

Can anyone name the key of this piece? Does anyone know a rule to help them identify key signatures containing flats? (The penultimate flat in the key signature is the tonic – with the exception of F major that has only a B flat.)

7. Rejoice in the Lord always

Music: Evelyn Tarner
arranged Esther Jones

Re - joice in the Lord__ al - ways and a - gain I say re - joice. Re -

-joice in the Lord__ al - ways and a - gain I say re - joice. Re -

-joice,____ re - joice,____ and a - gain I say re - joice. Re -

-joice,____ re - joice,____ and a - gain I say re - joice.

PIANO OSTINATO

Repeat ad lib.

To finish

8. Don't build your house on the sandy land

Information

The text of this song is based on Jesus's parable about the wise and foolish builders (Matthew 7). The wise man built his house on the rock and the foolish man on the sand. When a storm broke, the house of the foolish man fell down and was washed away but the house of the wise man stood firm. Through this story Jesus wanted to encourage his followers to build their lives on his teaching so that they could withstand the trials and troubles of life.

Teaching the song

It may be helpful to play the demonstration track on the CD to teach this song. It is very easy to pick up after a couple of hearings but difficult to read from the score. If you do play the recording, ask the singers to follow the music in their copies.

When you begin singing the piece, you may find that you need to practice bar 12 slowly in order to learn the chromatic inflection accurately. Once it is familiar, try singing it as a two-part round. When this is totally secure you can add the ostinato part as well.

Be creative

Younger singers may like to make up actions to perform with this song. It will help them to memorize the words and may also encourage them to sing out with greater confidence than they would if they were static.

Musical skills and understanding

The dotted quaver rhythm used throughout this song is known as 'swung quavers'. They are commonly used in jazz and blues music. Sometimes they are written as a triplet rhythm:

Swung rhythms are often much easier to learn by ear as they look complicated when written down. They should be sung quite lazily rather than with military precision.

8. Don't build your house on the sandy land

Words & music: Karen Lafferty
arranged Esther Jones

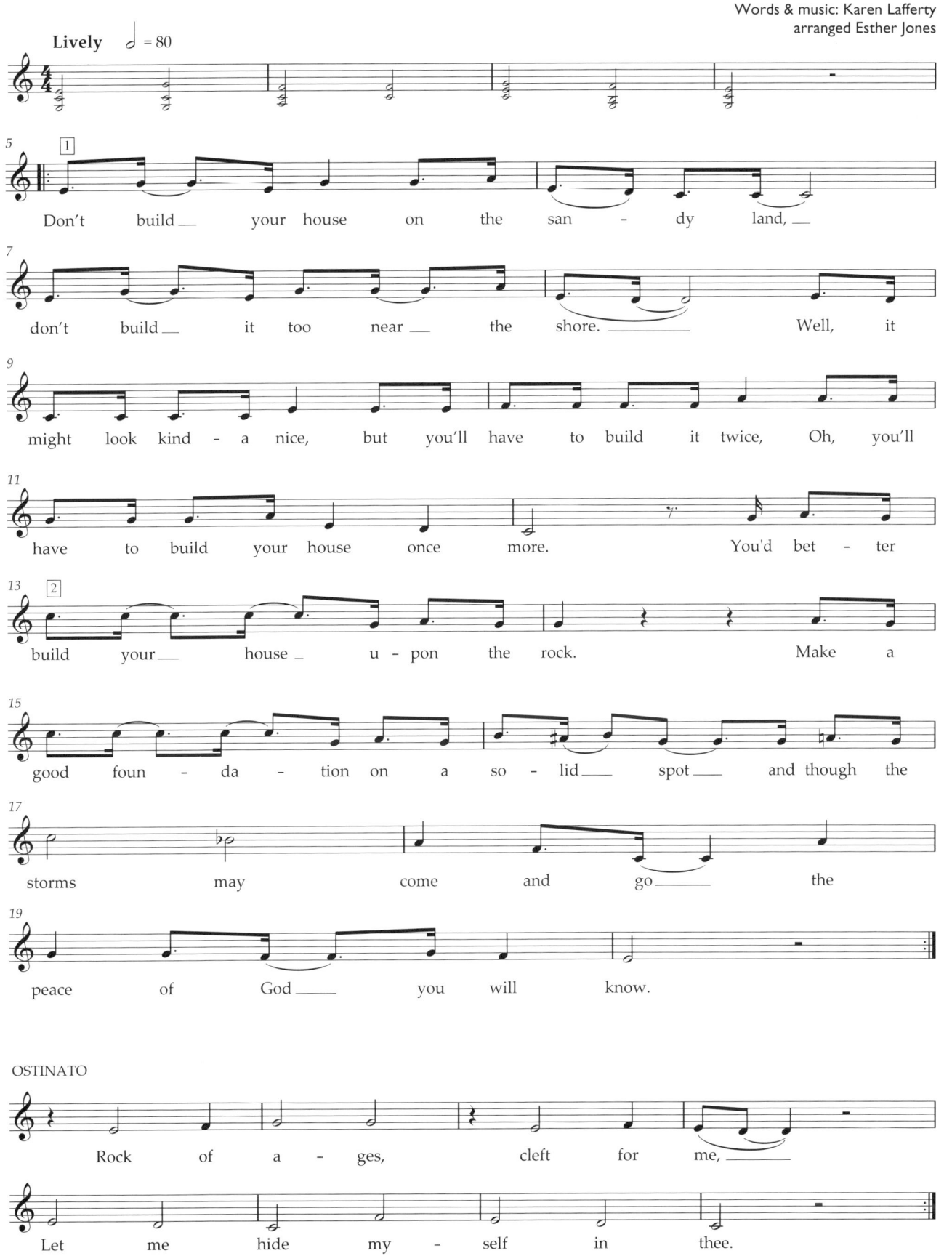

Lively ♩ = 80

Don't build ___ your house on the san - dy land, ___

don't build ___ it too near ___ the shore. ___ Well, it

might look kind - a nice, but you'll have to build it twice, Oh, you'll

have to build your house once more. You'd bet - ter

build your ___ house ___ u - pon the rock. Make a

good foun - da - tion on a so - lid ___ spot ___ and though the

storms may come and go ___ the

peace of God ___ you will know.

OSTINATO

Rock of a - ges, cleft for me, ___

Let me hide my - self in thee.

8. Don't build your house on the sandy land

Words & music: Karen Lafferty
arranged Esther Jones

rock.　　　　　Make a good foun - da - tion on a so - lid___ spot___ and though the

storms may come and go___ the peace of God you will know.

OSTINATO

Rock of a - ges, cleft for me,___ Let me hide my - self in thee.

9. Freedom train

Introduction

The African-American slaves were not allowed to practise traditional African religions and, over time, they adopted Christianity. On the whole, slaves were prevented from forming their own congregations for fear that they would rebel against their owners if allowed to meet on their own. Nonetheless, some slaves organized secret meetings, often at night, to worship together. It was at these meetings that preachers developed songs which became known as 'spirituals'. These songs drew both on African performance traditions and on hymns from the white churches.

Many spirituals, including this song, focus on the theme of freedom. It is an idea that has a double meaning. Not only do the worshippers sing of their journey toward spiritual freedom through faith, but the songs also express their hope for freedom from slavery.

Teaching the song

You can teach this song in a call and response pattern, two bars at a time. The words in the first four bars are a bit of a tongue-twister at speed and it may help to practise by saying them in rhythm a few times before you sing them. At a fast tempo singers should aim to be able to sing the first four bars in one breath.

To avoid singers accidentally singing in the rests in bars 5 and 7 you could ask them to nod or sniff at those moments – but don't let it become a habit otherwise it may occur in performance!

The last two bars have the trickiest rhythm. You need to make sure that this is accurate before you attempt singing the song as a round.

Younger singers will enjoy singing the 'Woo, woo' train noises. Ask them to imitate the sound of a train's whistle: they need to avoid tightening their throats and engage their support mechanism to produce a resonant sound. You can also use this type of sound in a warm-up to help develop the head voice.

Be creative

You can sing this as a round in two or four parts, accompanied by the piano or a cappella. You may also like to include the suggested vocal percussion parts or make up your own to start and end the song, to give the impression that a train is leaving the station and then arriving at its destination. Ask your singers for their ideas on how to perform the piece.

Musical skills and understanding

Can your singers identify the different note durations used in this piece? (It includes semiquavers, quavers, crotchets and minims, as well as crotchet and minim rests). Which is the shortest and which is the longest?

Can anyone identify the symbol over the last note of the vocal percussion part? And what does the dynamic marking below mean?

Ask your singers whether they notice anything about the pattern of notes that they sing in the first three bars of this song. (It outlines an F major chord, the key of the piece.)

9. Freedom train

Words & music: Spiritual

This old free-dom train is such a long time in a-com-ing, Now there's

none who can't af-ford it so you come and climb a-board it, sing-ing:

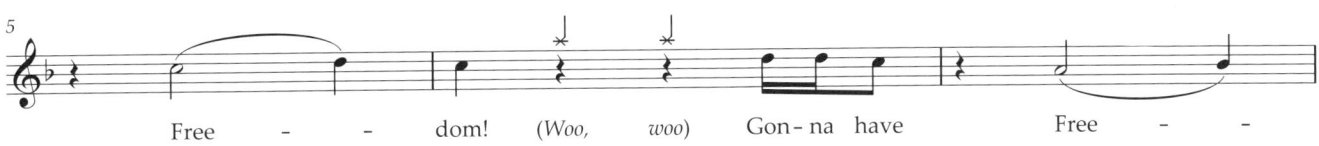

Free — dom! (*Woo, woo*) Gon-na have Free — —

-dom! (*Woo, woo*) Gon-na have Free-dom! Free-dom! Free-dom!

Repeat ad lib.

PIANO VAMP

Repeat ad lib.   *To finish*

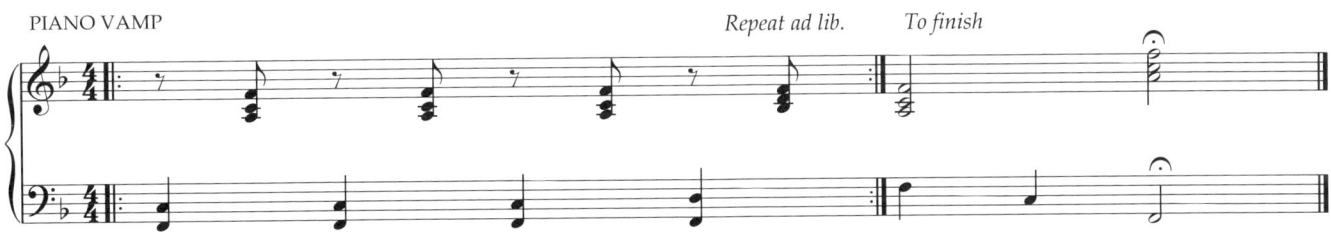

VOCAL PERCUSSION

Repeat ad lib.   *To finish*

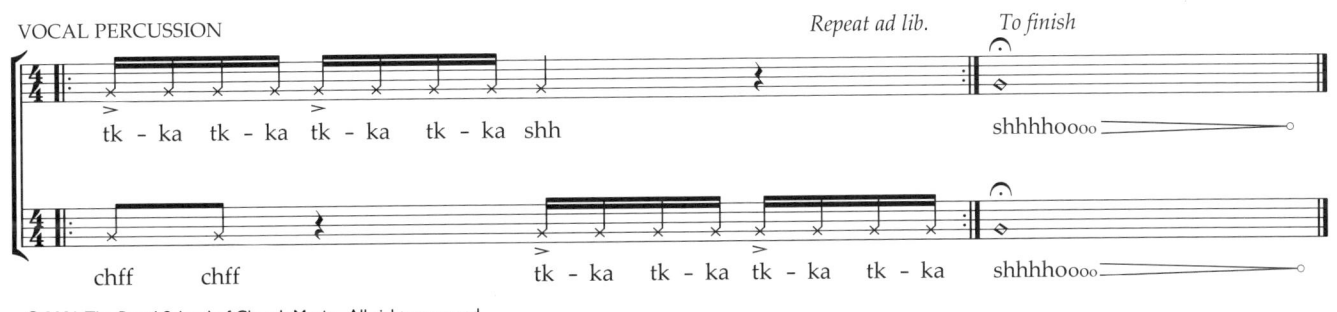

tk - ka tk - ka tk - ka tk - ka shh   shhhhoooo

chff   chff   tk - ka tk - ka tk - ka tk - ka   shhhhoooo

10. Now go in peace

Introduction

The melody of this song is a Caribbean folksong. The words have been written by Michael Mair. It can be used as a blessing at the end of a service or school assembly.

Preparation

One of the most interesting features of this song is its rhythm. You could prepare before singing by doing some clapping games:

- Ask singers to 'keep the beat in their feet' by treading lightly on the spot.

- Clap a number of rhythms and ask your singers to clap them back as an echo. Try to include some of the rhythms from the song (especially the syncopated rhythm in bar 3). Can they feel the way in which some rhythms work across the main beats of the bar?

- Ask other members of the group to lead the clapping – you could also try including other forms of body percussion such as finger clicks, slapping knees etc.

Teaching the song

The song starts on an off beat. If singers aren't sure about where to start the entry will probably be late, particularly if they don't take a breath early enough. You may need to count them in to begin with: suggest that they begin breathing at the beginning of your count.

Musical skills and understanding

What does syncopation mean? Can anyone identify the syncopated rhythms in this song?

The first two bars of the melody form a scalic pattern, moving in tones and semitones. What is the difference between a tone and a semitone? Can you identify the pattern of tones and semitones at the start of the piece?

10. Now go in peace

Words: Michael Mair

Music: Traditional Caribbean
arranged Michael Mair

11. Dona nobis pacem

Information

The Latin text 'Dona nobis pacem' means 'grant us peace'. This short round may therefore be used as a prayer response in times of war or on Remembrance Day.

Preparation

The melody of this song is made up of passages based on scales and arpeggios. It would help to practise these before attempting the piece.

1) Sing a scale of F major to the numbers 1–8.

2) Make up some patterns using the note numbers of the scale, to increase tonic awareness and to help singers gain familiarity with the different degrees of the scale:

1, 1 2 1, 1 2 3 2 1, 1 2 3 4 3 2 1, 1 2 3 4 5 4 3 2 1, 1 2 3 4 5 6 5 4 3 2 1 etc.

8, 8 7 8, 8 7 6 7 8, 8 7 6 5 6 7 8, 8 7 6 5 4 5 6 7 8 etc.

3) Teach singers to internalize sounds by devising patterns of notes that leave out one or more scale degrees. This will force them to think each of the missing notes in their heads in order to be able to pitch the next note that they sing:

1 2 3 4 5 6 7 8, 1 - 3 4 5 6 7 8, 1 2 - 4 5 6 7 8, 1 2 3 - 5 6 7 8, 1 2 3 4 - 6 7 8 etc.

1 2 3 4 5 6 7 8, - 2 3 4 5 6 7 8, - - 3 4 5 6 7 8, - - - 4 5 6 7 8, - - - - 5 6 7 8 etc.

4) Try singing patterns that make up arpeggiated chords:

1 3 5 8 5 3 1,   2 5 7 5 2,   2 4 6 4 2 etc.

Teaching the song

Now that the F major scale is familiar it will be easier to teach the opening bars of this song, which are based on arpeggiated chords. The passages of the song that move in stepwise motion are easy to sightread.

Musical skills and understanding

Ask singers to identify which passages are based on scales and which are based on chords. Can they name the chords outlined by the melody in bar 1, 2 and 23?

The widest leap in the melody of this song is an octave. Can they find two examples of an octave leap?

11. Dona nobis pacem

Words & music: Traditional

12. Hallelujah4

Information

This piece by Paul Ayres may be used as a musical exercise, warm-up or game, in performance as an introductory song, a participatory number with audience, or even in a church service as a gospel acclamation. It was first used in a children's singing workshop at the Foundling Museum in London, where they were able to see one of Handel's autograph scores of *Messiah* and read the first 'Hallelujah' from his own handwriting.

Preparation

Ask the singers to sing 'Hallelujah!' (without giving them any preparation or warning). They may well come up with the first melody here. Do they know who wrote it? Do they know any other pieces from *Messiah*? Or any other music by Handel?

Now teach the singers the four different 'Hallelujah' melodies below, clearly labelling each one as 'Hallelujah 1', 'Hallelujah 2' etc, and ask them to describe and compare the tunes.

Can they conduct the shapes of the melodies in the air? Do they notice that some syllables have two notes to them (no. 2: 'Halle*lu*jah', no. 3: '*Hallelujah*')? Practise singing them in various orders.

Now try singing each Hallelujah twice, with a rest in between. String together the four Hallelujahs, singing each one twice, with a rest in between the repeated pair, but without a rest when moving from no. 1 to no. 2, from no. 2 to no. 3, or from no. 3 to no. 4.

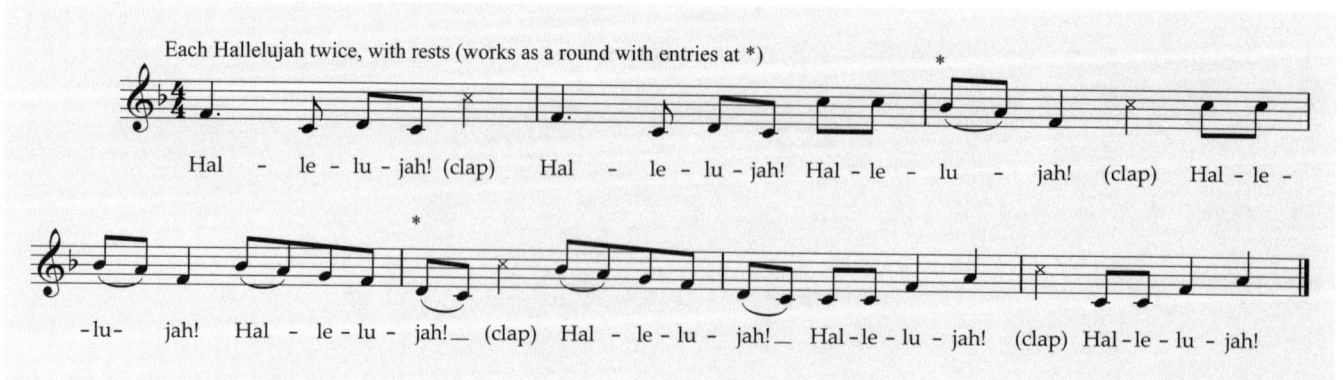

It's initially tricky, but once they have it, that's the basic principle of the piece covered.

Encourage your singers to play with this idea. For example, try the same process but with each Hallelujah sung three times, not twice. (How many Hallelujahs will they then sing?). Can the singers articulate the rest in any way, with a sniff, a foot stamp, or a clap? If they clap on each rest, and sing each Hallelujah three times, how many claps will the song have? And so on.

Teaching the song

Those who are used to reading music will probably find it much easier to learn from the score, rather than using the processes above, though one should always aim to perform this piece without looking down at the score.

To teach by rote or to memorize the complete 'piece' as written, first divide your singers into four teams, A, B, C and D (if you have a mixed-ability group, put the least experienced members in group A).

Then explain that the piece is in four sections:

1. INTRODUCTION
    Team A sings Hallelujah 1, Team B sings Hallelujah 2, etc, one after the other (with no rests).

2. MAIN SECTION
    Starting together:

    Team A sings Hallelujah 1 eight times, with a clap in between each;

    Team B sings Hallelujah 1 twice, then Hallelujah 2 six times, with a clap in between except where they change tune from no. 1 to no. 2;

    Team C sings Hallelujah 1 twice, then Hallelujah 2 twice, then Hallelujah 3 four times, with a clap in between except where they change tune from no. 1 to no. 2 and from no. 2 to no. 3;

    Team D sings each Hallelujah twice, following the same pattern.

3. MAIN SECTION 'DOUBLE'
    As main section above, but double the number of times they sing each Hallelujah, and with two claps instead of one.

4. CODA
    As introduction, but hold your last note until everyone has sung. Watch the conductor to finish the chord together.

12. Hallelujah4

12 MAIN SECTION 'DOUBLE'

CODA

13. Sing with me

Information

In 'Sing with me' composer Ken Burton celebrates the joy of singing together by combining three songs at once. Each song can be sung separately or together with one or more of the others. This piece is part of the gospel music tradition, which has its roots in the spirituals sung by the African-American slaves (see p. 34).

Teaching the song

Teach this song by rote in two-bar phrases starting with Voice I. Once you have sung through Voice I as call and response, ask your singers to sing it all the way through. Then go on to teach the other voice parts in the same way. Once all the parts are secure in unison, divide your singers into three groups and get them singing all the parts together simultaneously. Having done this you will need to decide with your singers how you will structure your performance of the song.

Using the voice well

There is a danger on words such as 'Sing' that your singers will try and close onto the 'ng' too quickly. Encourage them to keep the vowel sound open as long as possible. Even in bar 1 where the first note 'Sing' is relatively short ask your singers to create the most resonant sound possible.

In bar 9 (in both Voice I and II) the singers have the word 'me' over more than one note. Make sure they don't aspirate on each new note – you shouldn't hear 'me-he', just a smooth transition from one note to the next with no interruption to the vowel. If your singers find this hard (particularly in Voice II where they must rise up a fourth on the same vowel) ask them to try this adding a slide in between the two notes. Once they can achieve this smoothly, remove the slide but ask your singers to reproduce the same sense of connection between the notes.

Be creative

There are a number of different ways to perform this song. You could allocate one song to each group and start by singing each one separately before joining them together. Alternatively, you could sing it as a round with each group singing each song in succession. Invite your singers to help you decide how you want to perform it.

Musical skills and understanding

What key is this piece written in (with F♯ in the key signature)?

Can your singers find any notes that don't belong in this key – an 'accidental'? (e.g. in bar 7 there is a C♯).

13. Sing with me

Words & music: Ken Burton

SUGGESTED PERFORMANCE

Sing each song separately,
then go back to the beginning
and add each song on each successive verse.
However, feel at liberty to be creative with the structure.

Sing with me

Words & music: Ken Burton

Unison songs

14. Bring the children

◉ **Track 14**

Information

This song has been written by Bazil Meade, director of the London Community Gospel Choir. The text relates to Jesus's encounter with children in Judea, as recorded in Matthew 19. The disciples rebuke the children but Jesus welcomes them for prayer, explaining that the kingdom of God belongs to them.

Preparation

You may like to listen to and compare some recordings of gospel choirs and traditional cathedral or church choirs before learning this song. Ask your singers if they can hear what makes a gospel choir sound different from a traditional church or cathedral choir. What are the characteristics of each? Here are some examples:

Cathedral/traditional church choirs

- The vocal tone is as pure as possible and even throughout the vocal range.

- Notes are always hit exactly in the centre.

- Intervals between notes are negotiated as quickly as possible, with no slide between the notes.

Gospel choirs

- The vocal tone has more vibrato, and draws on a wider range of tonal colours for expressive purposes (e.g. breathy tone, powerful projection, a gravely, husky sound, etc.)

- There is a sense of freedom and relaxation in the singing: notes are not always struck immediately in the centre – the pitch is often 'bent' and intervals can be negotiated with a 'lazy feel' using slides on occasion.

Teaching the song

You can teach this song by rote, demonstrating the melody in two-bar phrases and asking your singers to imitate you. Remember to demonstrate this with a gospel feel, i.e. don't feel you have to hit each note precisely in the centre each time – feel free to add in small slides between notes (portamento), etc.

Make sure your singers understand how to follow the music (how many times the repeat happens, and where the music ends, for example). Then try singing the whole song through.

Be creative

As this song is in unison throughout, you could add some variety by allocating solos or small groups to sing the verses, and everyone could join in for the chorus. You might also like to perform the song in keeping with a gospel choir performance by adding some movement: gentle swaying and clicking your singers on the second and fourth beats of the bar, for example. But feel free to experiment – relax and move in a way that feels natural.

14. Bring the children

Words & Music: Bazil Meade
arranged Kit Perona-Wright

Bring the chil-dren to Je-sus now, let his

Spi – rit a-noint them while they are young. Teach them to love him in their

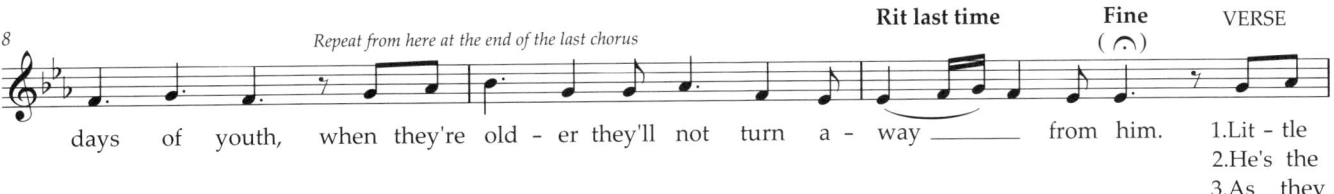

days of youth, when they're old – er they'll not turn a – way _____ from him.

1. Lit – tle
2. He's the
3. As they

ones	so	dear	in his ten – der care,	he wants their hearts and __ lives to share.
friend	to	have	as they grow in years	he'll guide them through all their hopes and fears.
find	true	faith	in his love they'll stay	he'll walk with them from __ day to day.

14. Bring the children

Words & Music: Bazil Meade
arranged Kit Perona-Wright

52

15. Now thank we all our God

Information

This song by Joanna Marsh is based on the text of the seventeenth-century German hymn 'Nun danket alle Gott'. It is suitable for Mothering Sunday and many other occasions of thanksgiving.

Preparation

The melody of this song is based on the E major scale. It would be helpful to sing this scale to the numbers 1 to 8 before starting work on it.

Now make up some patterns using the note numbers of the scale, to increase tonic awareness and to help singers gain familiarity with the different degrees of the scale:

1, 1 2 1, 1 2 3 2 1, 1 2 3 4 3 2 1, 1 2 3 4 5 4 3 2 1, 1 2 3 4 5 6 5 4 3 2 1 etc.

8, 8 7 8, 8 7 6 7 8, 8 7 6 5 6 7 8, 8 7 6 5 4 5 6 7 8 etc.

Next, teach your singers to internalize sounds by devising patterns of notes that leave out one or more scale degrees. This will force them to think each of the missing notes in their heads in order to be able to pitch the next note that they sing:

1 2 3 4 5 6 7 8, 1 - 3 4 5 6 7 8, 1 2 - 4 5 6 7 8, 1 2 3 - 5 6 7 8, 1 2 3 4 - 6 7 8 etc.

1 2 3 4 5 6 7 8, - 2 3 4 5 6 7 8, - - 3 4 5 6 7 8, - - - 4 5 6 7 8, - - - - 5 6 7 8 etc.

Can your singers work out the numbers of the scale degrees that they sing in bars 5–6 of 'Now thank we all our God'? (1 2 3 4 5 4 5 4 3 2 3 2 1). Ask them to sightread them.

Teaching the song

Although the voices sing in unison throughout this song, the choir needs to be divided into two equal groups. Like passing the baton in a relay race, each group needs to be ready to pick up the melody from the previous group. They need to make sure they breathe early otherwise their entry will be late.

Using the voice well

The first note of this song is quite low. Singers may need to work hard to find a resonant sound in this range of their voice. If they do not give it enough weight and length, it will not be heard.

Musical skills and understanding

The melody of this song moves mostly in steps of a tone or semitone but there are a few leaps. Can your singers identify these leaps and name the intervals (e.g. a perfect fourth between the first two notes)?

15. Now thank we all our God

Words: Martin Rinkart (1586-1649)
translated Catherine Winkworth (1827-1878)

Music: Joanna Marsh

15. Now thank we all our God

Words: Martin Rinkart (1586-1649)
translated Catherine Winkworth (1827-1878)

Music: Joanna Marsh

may this boun-teous God through all__ our life be near__ us,

with e - ver joy-ful hearts and bless-

- ed peace to cheer__ us;

and keep us in his grace, and guide__ us when per - plexed;

and

free us from all ills,   in this world and the   next!

All   praise and thanks to God   the Fa -

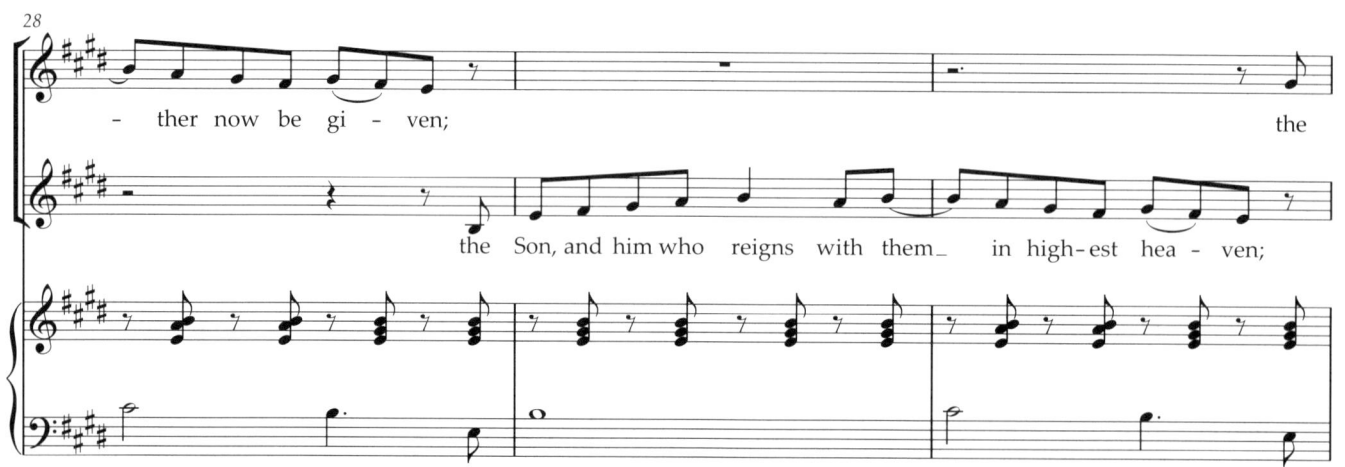

- ther now be gi - ven;   the

the   Son, and him who   reigns with them_   in high-est hea - ven;

one e-ter-nal God, whom earth___ and heav'n a-dore;

for   thus it was, is now   and shall___ be e-ver-

be   e-ver-more,

p

- more,

subito f

be e-ver-more!

subito f

pp

be e-ver-more,

be e-ver-more!

subito f

16. The fruits of the land

 Track 16

Information

This song by David Ogden is suitable for harvest or other times of the year where the theme is God's gifts, creation or service to others.

Preparation

Before you start make sure your singers understand the geography of the piece. At the end of each verse they return to the refrain and then, after the final refrain, they must jump from bar 11 to the Coda at the end of the piece.

Teaching the song

Start by teaching the refrain and sing it through a few times until it is secure. Next, work on the verses. The rhythms of each verse are slightly different so you will need to practise each one separately. The harmony in the coda is optional but is simple enough to be managed by most choirs. Rehearse the upper part separately and then put it with the lower part, which remains on the tune.

Using the voice well

The first note of this song is quite low. Singers may need to work hard to find a resonant sound in this range of their voice. If they do not give it enough weight and length it will not be heard.

The last note of each verse is six beats long. Singers need to maintain their breath support throughout this note in order to keep the sound vibrant. Experiment with it by asking them to crescendo or diminuendo through the note – or both. Can they keep the sound alive even while changing dynamic?

Musical skills and understanding

Can your singers translate or give a description of the following musical terms that are marked in the score? *A tempo* (bar 5), *coda* (bar 26), *poco rall* (bar 25), *div.* (bar 27).

The tempo of the piece is marked crotchet = 96. What does this mean?

16. The fruits of the land
A new harvest song

Words: Helena Hobbs

Music: David Ogden

16. The fruits of the land
A new harvest song

Words: Helena Hobbs

Music: David Ogden

gave us the earth, _____ pro - vi - ded the seed _ Of things that would grow to ful -
peo - ple give time _ when they help for our sake, And o - thers are gift - ed at
give us the chance to help o - thers in need _ To give of our - selves _____ in

- fil ev - 'ry need. To nur - ture these gifts _ he _ brought us to birth So we
things they can make. God gave us these gifts _ which he spread through the land So we
ev - 'ry good deed. We thank you, O Lord, _____ that we play a part __ And _

bring you, we bring you the fruits of the earth. _____
bring you, we bring you the fruit of our hands. _____
bring you, and bring you the fruit of our hearts. _____

poco rall.　　　　CODA　　　　slower
　　　　　　　　　　　　　　　　　div.

___ You __ We bring you the fruits of the land. _

17. The Lord is my light

⊙ **Track 17**

Information

The text of 'The Lord is my light' is based on Psalm 27. This jazz-infused setting by John Bell is catchy and memorable.

Preparation

The song is based on the additive rhythm: dotted crotchet, dotted crotchet, crotchet. If you subdivide it into quavers you can count it: 1 2 3, 1 2 3, 1 2. Ask your singers to clap the rhythm while counting this pattern. You could also ask them to make up an action in time to the rhythm to help externalize it.

The melody in the refrain contains lots of repeated notes (e.g. three As in bars 1 and 3). It can be surprisingly difficult to keep repeated notes in tune when you change vowel sounds. To prepare for this you could ask your singers to sing these (or other) exercises that contain different vowel sounds:

In the first exercise the quavers should be sung staccato. They need to be well-supported with a relaxed rather than tight throat.

Exercise 2 should be sung legato with no break in the sound between the notes. Sing it slowly enough for singers to be able to check that the pitch of each repeated note does not change.

Teaching the song

Teach the refrain first. Even at this early stage you should encourage your choir to end their phrases together. They will need to take care to place the 't' of 'light' together in bars 6 and 14 and the 'd' of 'afraid' in bar 19.

The last four bars of each verse should be sung in one breath (e.g. 'when my enemies smell the scent of vict'ry they shall stumble and fall'). Try to crescendo through this last phrase so it builds towards the chorus.

Using the voice well

When singing descending scales, as happens in the verse of this song, the pitch often goes flat. It may help for the conductor to make an upwards gesture as the pitch descends – or for the singers to do this themselves as they sing. An upturned palm travelling upwards should help them maintain their breath support to the end of the phrase and keep the sound bright. Alternatively, ask singers to mime lifting a heavy box from waist to chest height as they sing this phrase: this will encourage them to engage their support mechanism.

17. The Lord is my light

Lux Mea

Music: John Bell

With energy

VOICE

The

Lord is my light, my light and sal - va - tion. Whom shall I

fear? Whom shall I fear? The Lord is my light, my light and sal -

except last time | *last time*

- va - tion. Why should I be a - fraid? —— ——

1. When the powers of e - vil move to - wards me, —— when my ve - ry flesh is un - der threat,

D.S.

when my e - ne - mies smell the scent of vict - r'y they shall stum - ble and fall. —— The

2. Should a mighty army camp around me,
   still my heart would register no fear.
   Though a war were waged,
   though it raged against me
   I'd trust God and stand firm.

3. One thing through it all my soul is seeking:
   to live all my life within God's house;
   there to spend my days,
   gazing at God's beauty
   while at one with my Lord.

4. God protects me in the time of trouble,
   shelters me yet sets me on a rock.
   Safe from every harm,
   safe from all that threatens
   I will sing and rejoice.

17. The Lord is my light

Lux Mea

Music: John Bell

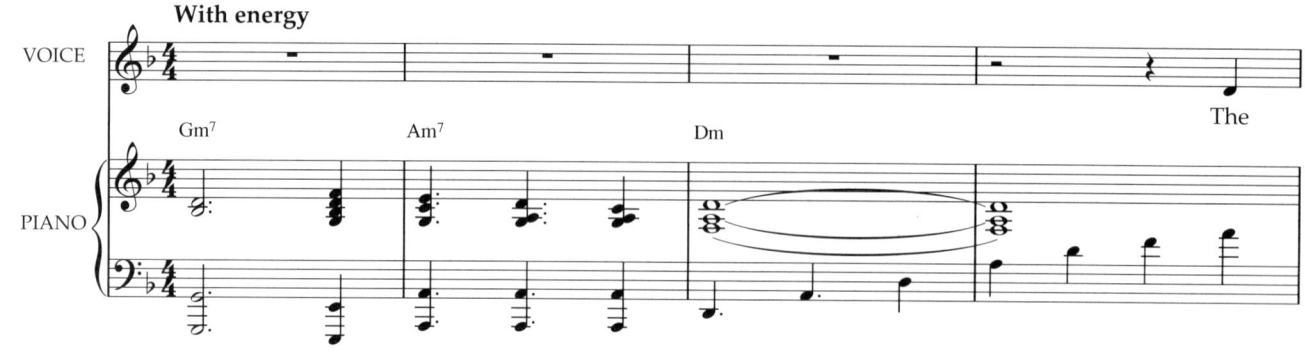

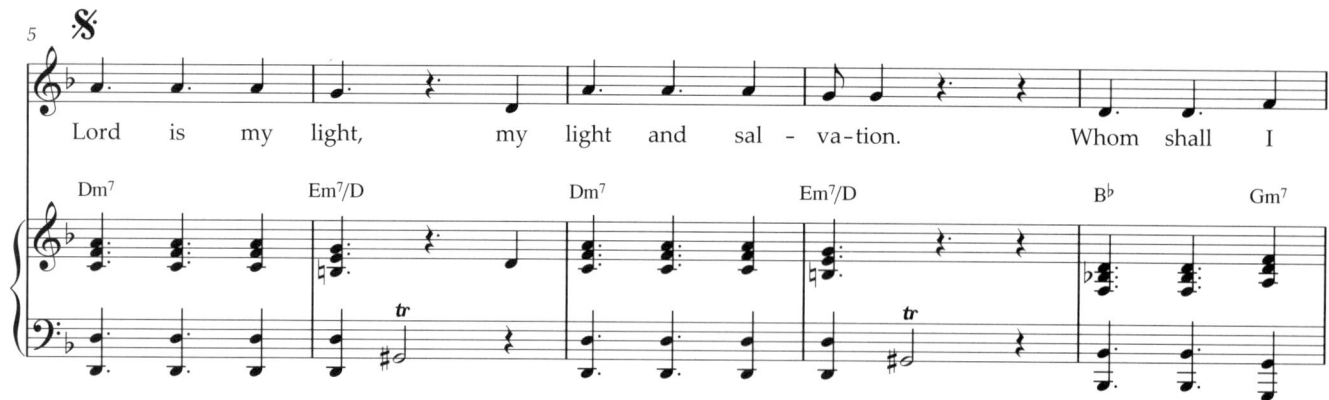

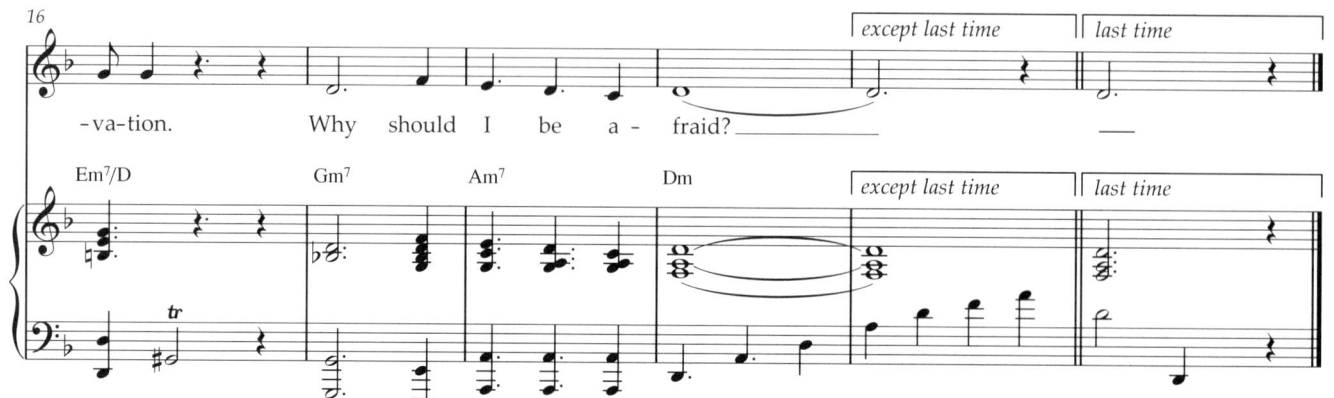

1. When the powers of e - vil move to-wards me, _____ when my ve - ry flesh is un-der threat,

D.S.

when my e - ne - mies smell the scent of vict - r'y they shall stum - ble and fall. _____ The

2. Should a mighty army camp around me,
   still my heart would register no fear.
   Though a war were waged,
   though it raged against me
   I'd trust God and stand firm.

3. One thing through it all my soul is seeking:
   to live all my life within God's house;
   there to spend my days,
   gazing at God's beauty
   while at one with my Lord.

4. God protects me in the time of trouble,
   shelters me yet sets me on a rock.
   Safe from every harm,
   safe from all that threatens
   I will sing and rejoice.

18. I will sing a song of love

●   **Track 18**

Information

'I will sing a song of love' considers why we sing praise to God and ends with a reminder that through song we can join in with the music of heaven.

Teaching the song

Young or inexperienced singers will find it difficult to sightread words, rhythm and pitch at the same time. You could use this song as sightreading practice, isolating these different elements and then putting them together. First ask singers to clap or speak the text of the first phrase in rhythm. Next ask them to read the pitches in free rhythm. Lastly, ask them to sing the phrase in rhythm (this could be to 'ah' at first, with the text added at the final stage).

Using the voice well

For the words of the chorus to make sense, you need to sing four bars to one breath. Your singers will need to keep the sound travelling on the longer notes (e.g. 'love' in bar 6) in order to keep it alive. It may help to make a small crescendo on these notes to maintain a sense of momentum.

In bars 21–22 the melody covers a wide range of notes. Make sure that it is still sung with a sense of line rather than chopped up into single notes. To enable this, first practice this phrase on a single vowel, e.g. 'ah' or 'oo'. Ask singers to slide between the notes to connect them. Gradually speed up the slides so that they can't be heard but the sound stays connected. When you add the text back in, try to keep a legato sound by making the vowels as long as possible.

Musical skills and understanding

The rhythm in bar 5 occurs in several other places in the song. Can anyone see where?

This song is in D major. Can anyone identify any notes that are not usually found it this key (e.g. F natural in bar 27 etc.)?

What does *D.S. al Fine* mean (written above the last bar of the verse)?

18. I will sing a song of love

Named and known

Music: John Bell
adapted Esther Jones

Brightly

VOICE

I will sing a song of love to the one who first loved me, and I'll sing it as a child of God who is named and known and free. For the love of God is good, it is broad and deep and long, and a-bove all else that mat-ters God is wor-thy of my song. 1. And I will not sing a-lone but with earth and sky and sea, for cre-a-tion raised its voice well in ad-vance of me. I will

2. And I'll sing with every soul,
   every language, every race,
   which proclaims this world is good
   for God has blessed this place.

3. And I'll sing for what is right
   and against all that is wrong,
   because God is never neutral
   who inspires my song.

4. As I bring to God my joy,
   so I'll bring to God my pain,
   for there is no hurt which God
   requires me to retain.

5. While my life on earth still runs,
   may my song to God be given,
   till through grace I join the harmony
   of all in heaven.

18. I will sing a song of love

Named and known

Music: John Bell
adapted Esther Jones

Brightly

VOICE

PIANO

I will

sing a song of love___ to the one who first loved me,___ and I'll

sing it as a child of God who is named and known and free.___ For the

love of God is good,___ it is broad and deep and long,___ and a-

-bove all else that mat-ters God is___ wor - thy___ of my song.___ **Fine**

1. And I will not sing a - lone___ but with earth and sky and sea,___ for cre-

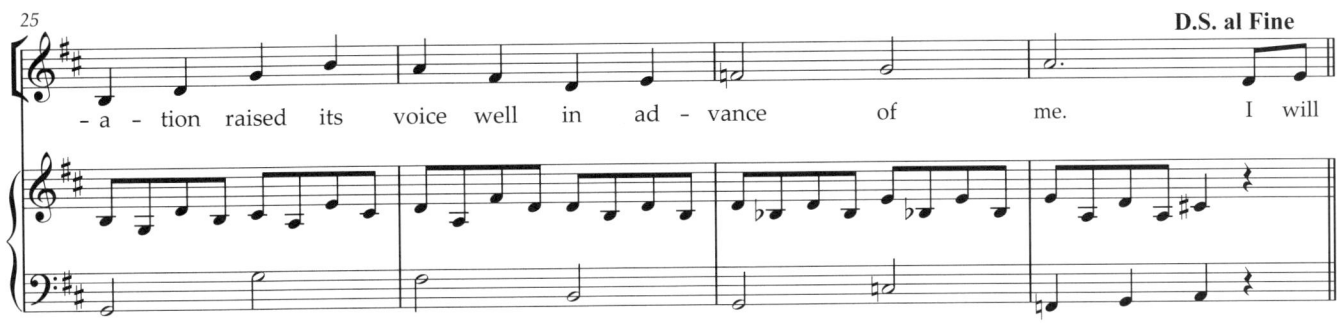

D.S. al Fine

- a - tion raised its voice well in ad - vance of me. I will

2. And I'll sing with every soul,
   every language, every race,
   which proclaims this world is good
   for God has blessed this place.

3. And I'll sing for what is right
   and against all that is wrong,
   because God is never neutral
   who inspires my song.

4. As I bring to God my joy,
   so I'll bring to God my pain,
   for there is no hurt which God
   requires me to retain.

5. While my life on earth still runs,
   may my song to God be given,
   till through grace I join the harmony
   of all in heaven.

19. A blessing for Mother's Day

Information

This blessing would make an ideal ending for a service on Mothering Sunday. It reminds us that, although we usually refer to God as our heavenly Father, he also displays maternal characteristics.

Preparation

Your singers will need good breath control to help them sing through the long phrases and negotiate the wide leaps which appear in the melody. You might like to do some breathing exercises with your singers before teaching this song, to get them used to taking a good deep (relaxed) breath and then controlling the expulsion of air very carefully (e.g. breathing in to four counts and then hissing or humming for eight counts). You can gradually increase the number of counts to which the singers are expelling air. Make sure the tone they produce is even – this will require good breath control.

You may also like to use the following exercise as a warm-up at the start of your rehearsal, moving the pitch up a semitone on each repeat.

Make sure that the note at the end of the second bar is as flat as possible. Ask your singers to make it really 'bluesy'!

They will need to use plenty of breath support as they negotiate the seventh between 'bless us' and 'now' in the third bar of the exercise. If they find this jump difficult, add a slide between the notes so they keep the tone connected. When they can do this successfully, omit the slide.

Once they are secure with the notes of this exercise, ask your singers to breathe after the first bar, and then go through the rest of the exercise in one breath (when they can breathe again on the rest before repeating back to the beginning). This will become more tricky once you have moved the pitch up a few times – they will need to take a deep breath each time to help them sing the highest note (which comes near the end of the phrase) in tune and with good tone.

Teaching the song

It is helpful for your singers to follow the music while learning this song, but demonstrate the melody to them four bars at a time and ask them to repeat what you have sung. They may need to hear certain sections of the melody more than once to help them internalize the syncopations and some of the wider interval leaps (e.g. 'bless us' bars 7–8, and 'may God who broods as a mother' bars 12–14). The final phrase of the melody will already be familiar to them from the vocal exercise used in your preparation.

Once your singers are secure with the notes, go through and decide where each of the phrases lie, and where your singers should breathe. Ask them to mark these breathing points in their music. It will also be helpful to decide which points in each phrase they should be aiming for – which words need special emphasis? Are there particular notes in the melody which feel as if they want to be brought out more than the others? Decide these together with your singers and mark them into the score. All this will help them with their breath management and will produce a more sensitive and mature performance of the song.

Using the voice well

The long phrases of this song demand good breath control. If your singers find that they cannot sustain whole phrases, ask them to 'stagger' their breathing by taking a breath at a different place from their neighbour so that the overall sound is continuous.

The melody includes several wide leaps. Encourage your singers to maintain a legato sound even when the melody moves by leap rather than step. It is helpful to isolate these moments and rehearse them slowly several times until they feel natural and comfortable for the singers.

Musical skills and understanding

What key is the piece written in? (two flats in the key signature).

From the last note of bar 13 to the first note of bar 14 the melody descends by a large interval. Can your singers name the interval?

What does *tutti* mean? (bar 24)

19. A blessing for Mother's Day

Music: Joanna Marsh

19. A blessing for Mother's Day

Music: Joanna Marsh

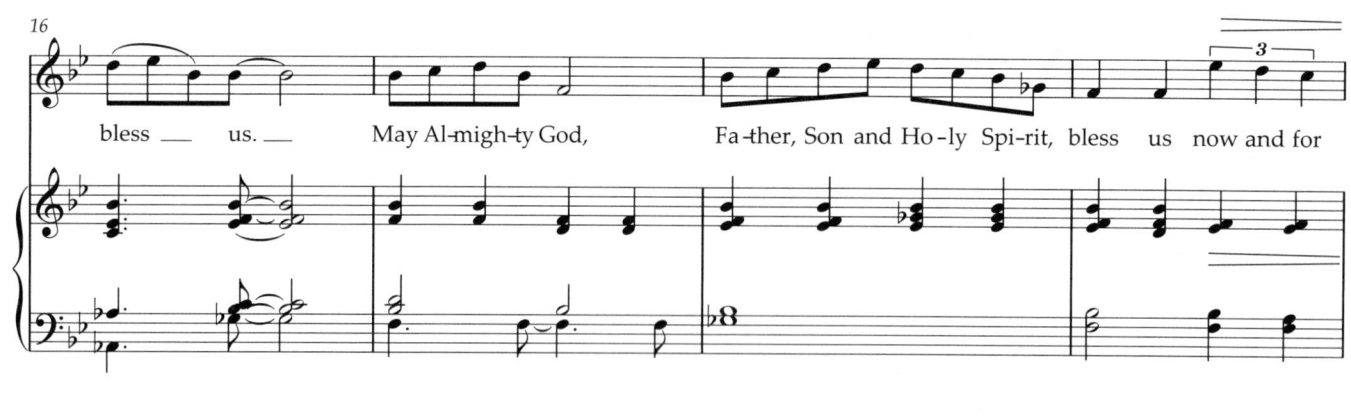

bless ___ us. ___   May Al-migh-ty God,   Fa-ther, Son and Ho-ly Spi-rit, bless us now and for

e - ver.

TUTTI
May ___ God, ___ who gave ___ birth to all ___ cre - a - tion, ___ bless ___

___ us. ___   May ___ God, who be-came in - car - nate ___ by an earth-ly

mo - ther, bless _____ us. ___ May ___ God, who broods as a mo-

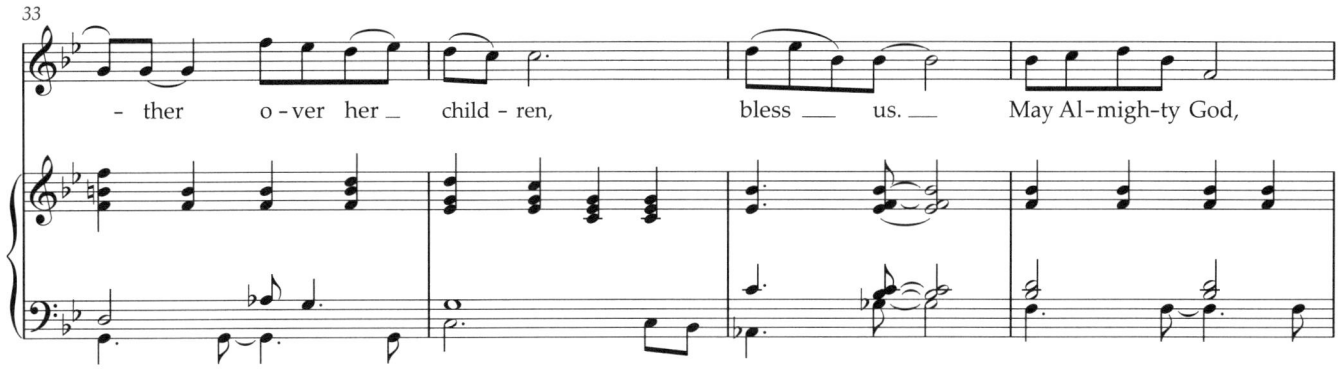

- ther o - ver her ___ child - ren, bless ___ us. ___ May Al - migh - ty God,

Fa ther, Son and Ho-ly Spi - rit, bless us now and for e - ver.

SEMI-CHORUS
mp

rit. *p*

May Al-migh ty God, Fa ther, Son and Ho - ly Spi - rit, bless us now and for e - ver.

mp rit.

p

Unison with descant

20. O when the saints

Information

This well-known song comes from the gospel tradition. The text, based on imagery from the book of Revelation, refers to Christ's Second Coming. The saints mentioned in the song include all believers marching on the way to the kingdom of heaven.

Teaching the song

This song is so well-known that it will require little rehearsal, but you will need to allow some time for working on the descant part.

Make sure the choir know when to enter after the piano introduction. You could help by counting the rests with them the first time through and then asking them to do it internally thereafter. Encourage them to prepare by taking a breath at the start of the bar: if they snatch a breath just before they come in they are liable to be late.

Encourage the singers on the descant part to 'feel' rather than count the rhythm for their first entry. It may help them to begin by singing the start of the melody line followed by the start of the descant part (this will also ensure that they find their first note). Once it is secure, ask them to stop singing the melody and instead to think it in their heads before they come in. If they listen to the start of the melody before taking a breath their entry is likely to be late, so remind them to start breathing early!

It may be helpful to rehearse the 'yeah' at the end of the song in isolation before putting it back into context. (You will need to decide in advance whether you want it to be in a stage whisper or shouted.) Count four aloud in tempo and ask your singers to say 'yeah' on the last beat of the bar. Once the ensemble is tight, sing through the whole of the last verse.

Musical skills and understanding

What is a *glissando*? You will hear one played on the piano in the last verse of this song. How do you achieve the same effect with your voice?

Listen to the piano part in the introduction. Can your singers describe the pattern of notes in the bass? (It moves down in semitones, with octave leaps in between, making a chromatic scale.)

What is the interval between the first two notes of the melody? Is it major or minor?

20. O when the saints

Spiritual
arranged Esther Jones

20. O when the saints

Spiritual
arranged Esther Jones

21. Amazing grace

●   **Track 21**

Information

This lively arrangement of *Amazing grace* is in a blues style. The hymn was written in the eighteenth century by John Newton, who worked on a slave ship. During a violent storm at sea he began to wrestle with his conscience and turned to the Bible for answers. He was inspired by the story of the prodigal son in Luke 15, the themes of which he takes up in his famous hymn. Later in his life he helped to influence law makers to abolish the slave trade within British colonies and emancipate the slaves held there.

Teaching the song

There are several different variations of this melody. Test your singers' music reading skills by asking them to stick to the score rather than just singing the version that is most familiar to them.

When teaching the descant, ask your singers to sing the start of the verse and then stop on the first note of the descant. Once secure, ask them to think the melody line in their heads in order to help them find their note and only sing the descant part.

Take care of tuning in the descant in bar 11. If you want to rehearse this bar slowly to work on intonation, sing it down an octave initially so as not to tire the singers' voices. They will have no problem singing it at pitch when you ask them to.

Using the voice well

In bar 13 the singers on the descant part may find it helpful to add a silent 'h' at the start of the word 'Alleluia'. This will help them to get the air flowing so that they can glide in smoothly, rather than accenting the note with a glottal stop.

Be creative

If the choir are to perform the song to an audience rather than singing it as a congregational hymn, think about how to achieve variety and contrast between the verses. You can do this by changing the dynamics or by giving a verse to a soloist or semichorus.

Musical skills and understanding

In 12/8 there are twelve quavers in a bar divided into four dotted crotchet beats. When subdividing the beat, count '1-and-a, 2-and-a, 3-and-a, 4-and-a'. It is this that gives the arrangement the 'swung' feel.

Can you identify the ornament in the first bar of the piano introduction in the right hand? (It is an *acciaccatura* or crushed note).

In bars 11–16, can you identify where the descant part moves by semitone and where it moves by a tone?

The coda (end section) at bar 22–24 of this arrangement quotes another piece of music. Do you know what it is or who it is by? (*Rhapsody in blue* by Gershwin).

What do the figure 2s over the notes mean? (These are called duplets and indicate that two notes are to be sung in the time of three.)

21. Amazing grace

Music: Traditional
arranged Esther Jones

21. Amazing grace

Music: Traditional
arranged Esther Jones

13
Al - - - le - - - lu - - - ia, let's
once was lost but now am found, was
pre - cious did that grace ap - pear the
grace that brought me safe thus far, and
no less days to sing God's praise, than
17
1. 2. 3.
sing God's
blind but now I see. 2.'Twas
hour I first be - lieved. 3.Through
grace will lead me home. 4.When
when we first be -
21
4.
rit.
praise.
gun.

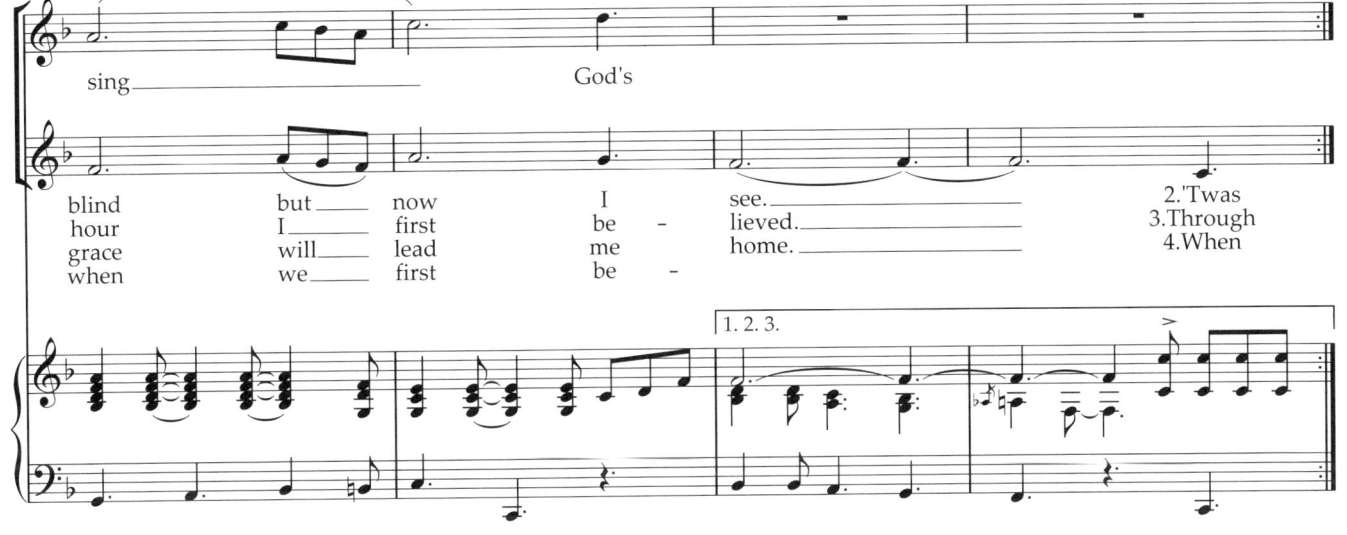

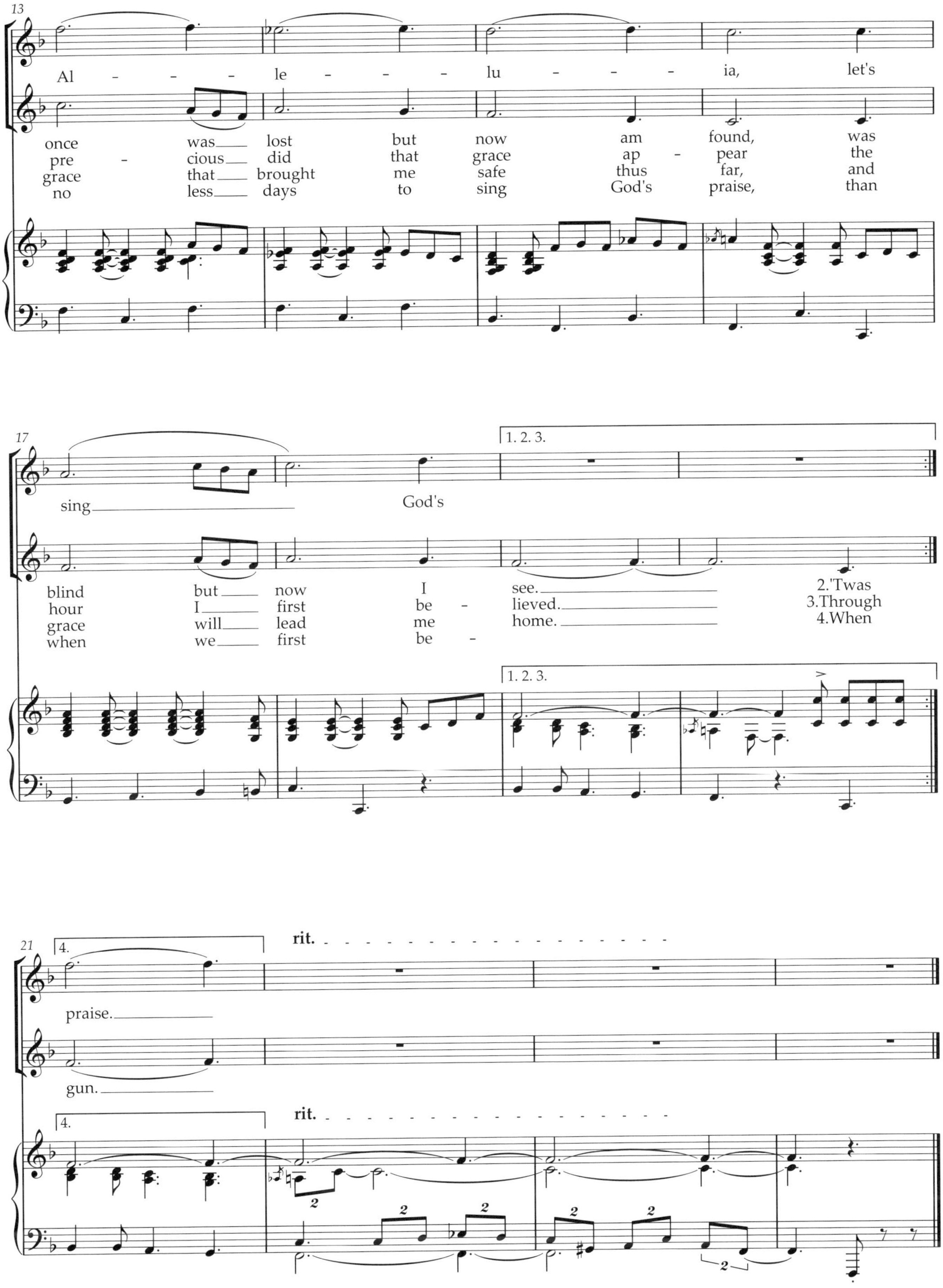

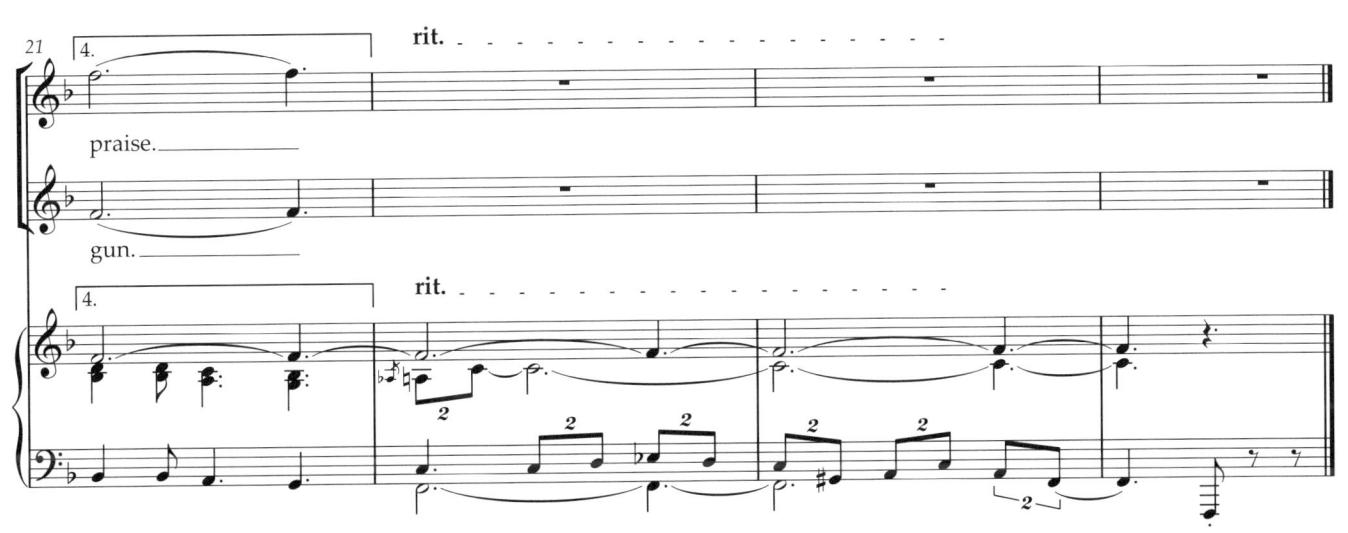

22. Prayer of St Benedict

● **Track 22**

Information

The text of this song is a paraphrase of a prayer by St Benedict. Benedict was an Italian monk who lived in the sixth century. He founded a monastry in Monte Cassino in Italy that became the roots of the Church's monastic system. He wrote a Rule to direct his community which focused on prayer and work. This Rule is still followed by many monasteries today.

Preparation

This song is mainly in 3/4 but there are several changes of time signature in the piece. Go through and identify where these occur so the singers are prepared for them.

There are bars in 2/4 and 4/4 as well as 3/4. To help the singers understand the difference between them and introduce the beat patterns used by the conductor, practise conducting in these different time signatures.

When introducing beat patterns, the singers may find it useful to hold out their left arm across their body at elbow height, with their palm facing down. This forms the base point for their conducting gestures in the right hand. The downbeat of each bar, whatever the time signature, should move from around shoulder height down to make contact with the wrist of the left hand. The upbeat should always return to the starting position. When conducting in two, the right hand should curve slightly to the right after brushing the wrist of the left and then travel back up. When beating three in a bar, the right hand should touch the wrist of the left hand on the downbeat, travel out to the right across the knuckles on the second beat and brush the fingertips on the upbeat. In four, the right hand should make contact with the wrist, elbow, knuckles then fingertips of the left hand. The point at which the right hand makes contact with the left should coincide exactly with the beats in the bar. Travel between the beats should remain steady and fluid.

Once the beating patterns are familiar the singers should take away their left hands but still imagine it is there, so that the downbeat falls in the same place each time and there is no confusion as to which direction each beat travels (avoiding the common problem of beating four in the bar back-to-front).

When the singers can confidently beat in two, three and four, ask them to try to conduct bars 8–12 or 28–34 of this song. Can they move fluidly from one time signature to the other?

Teaching the song

Start by singing the first verse through on an 'oo' sound. Encourage your singers to sing legato even when there are wide leaps. Also, make sure that they breathe at the appropriate places even at this stage. When the melody is familiar, sing through verses one and two with the text. You will need to practise placing the final consonants together in bars 12 and 18. You can help by telling the choir on which beat (or half beat) to place the consonant. They will need to count, watch the conductor and listen to each other in order to get it precisely together.

The melody of verse three is identical to the previous verses, with the exception of the last two bars where the rhythm changes. Ask your singers to compare bars 21–22 with bars 31–33 and spot the differences.

Rehearse the final line of the verse and the coda before going through the whole of verse three from the start.

Finally, work on the descant. As it starts in canon with the melody the first phrase will already be familiar.

Using the voice well

In bar 10 and equivalent places in the other verses, the singers will need to take a quick breath as marked. To prevent it being a tense gasp for air, the conductor and accompanist should allow enough time for the end of the previous word to be properly formed and for a relaxed intake of breath. Providing this is done in a musical way it should not disrupt the flow of the melodic line. Start by practising this passage under tempo and gradually speed it up. Encourage your singers to take a low, deep breath at this point.

In order to cement the ensemble you may need to rehearse bar 21 slowly to ensure that on the word 'take', the change of vowel (ay-ee) and the 'k' are sounded together. Choral singers usually elongate the first vowel in a diphthong and leave the change until just before they leave the note. The 'k' should also be left as late as possible, but you need to avoid the text sounding like 'tay kand share' by putting a small glottal stop at the start of 'and'.

Musical skills and understanding

Can anyone identify the loudest and quietest passages in the piece? (Hint: look for the *fff* and *ppp* markings.)

At the start of the last verse 'Feet to walk on sacred earth', the vocal line divides into two parts. What is the relationship between the two parts? (They sing exactly the same music but in canon until bar 29 where the upper part does something different).

What does the metronome mark over bar 1 mean? Can anyone think of a suitable Italian term to describe the mood and tempo of the piece?

22. Prayer of St Benedict

Words: Jenni Lee Boyden & Rusty Edwards
based on the Prayer of St Benedict

Music: Jon Payne

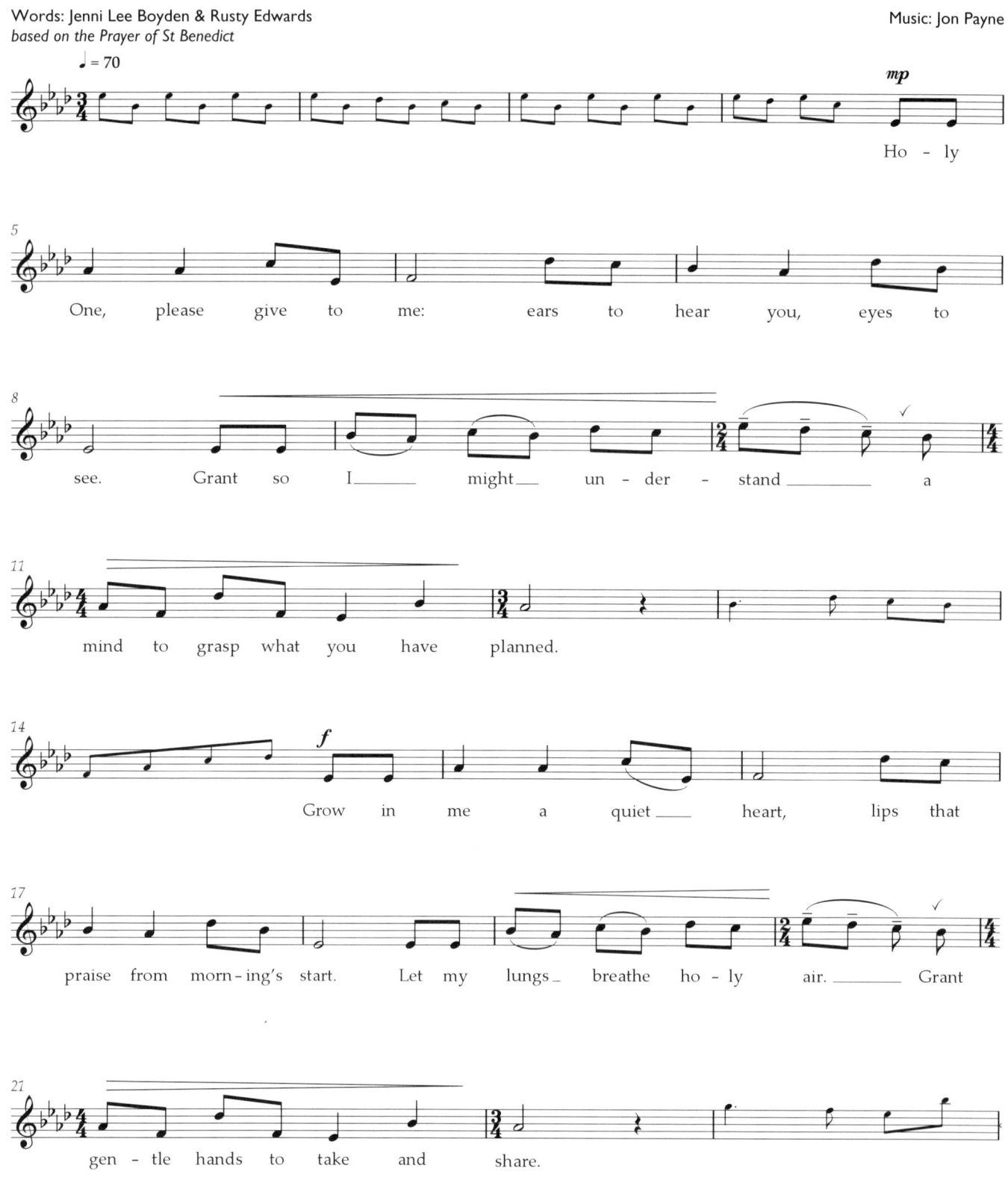

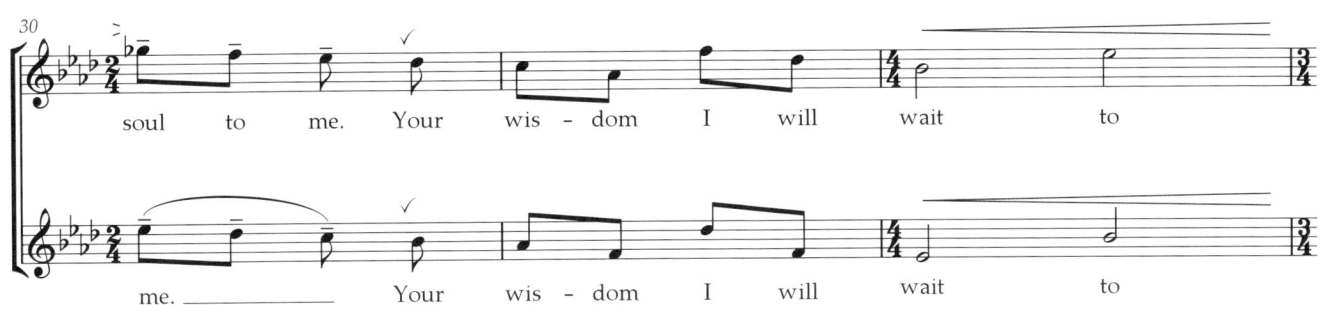

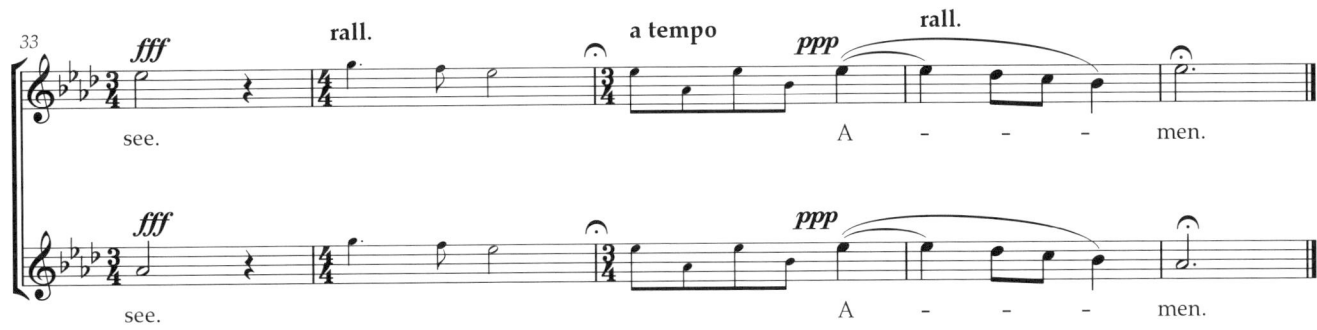

For Nigel Stark and the choristers of St Alphege Church, Solihull

22. Prayer of St Benedict

Words: Jenni Lee Boyden & Rusty Edwards
based on the Prayer of St Benedict

Music: Jon Payne

heart, lips that praise from morn-ing's start. Let my

lungs _ breathe ho - ly air. _____ Grant gen - tle hands to take and

share. Feet to

VOICE 1
walk on sa - cred earth; spi - rit
Feet to walk on sa - cred earth; spi - rit seek - ing for your

23. God the singer

Information

The Old Testament prophet Zephaniah refers to God singing over his people. This piece, with words by Peter Davison, encourages us to unite together and join in the Lord's song.

Preparation

Make sure your singers know how to count the rests in the introduction. When musicians have more than one bar of rests to count they usually count the beats in this pattern:

1 2 3 4, **2** 2 3 4, **3** 2 3 4, **4** 2 3 4 etc.

In this piece the singers will need to count up to **8** 2 3 and then enter on the fourth beat of the bar. Practise it once or twice with either you or everyone counting aloud, then ask your singers to count it in their heads (without tapping a foot, nodding their heads or counting on their fingers!). You might like to try this exercise with some other pieces as well, to check that everyone has understood the principles and is able to apply them to other songs.

Teaching the song

Try singing the first verse of this song on an open-mouthed hum (ng) making each phrase as smooth as possible. Try the same exercise again on an 'ah' sound. Once all the notes are correct and the singers have a sense of the shape of each phrase, add the text.

Verse two is similar to the first verse but has a few notable differences. Can your singers identify what these are? Try sightreading this verse: remember to watch out for repeated notes. Everyone assumes that staying on the same note is easy but singers often don't notice when to stick on the same pitch while they are sightreading!

There is an optional descant for the third verse. Go through the descant by itself before attempting to put it together with the melody. However, bear in mind that as each phrase of the descant starts in unison with the melody this will help those on the descant find the first notes of each phrase.

Using the voice well

Watch out for the diphthongs on 'voice' and 'rejoice' in the third verse. The singers should elongate the first vowel sound (aw) and then change to the second (ee) just before the consonant. If the whole choir try to make the same vowel sounds, the overall sound will be blended and together.

Musical skills and understanding

The metronome mark puts the tempo at 120 crotchets a minute. By looking at the second hand on a clock or watch, can you tap the pulse at this rate? Can you conduct four at the same speed? (It will help to keep the movements small and compact.)

This song starts in B flat major but changes key before the last verse. What key does it change to in bar 55?

The descant part starts in bar 54. In a number of places the descant is in unison with the melody part. Can you identify where this occurs?

God the Singer

Words: Peter Davison

Music: David Ogden

96

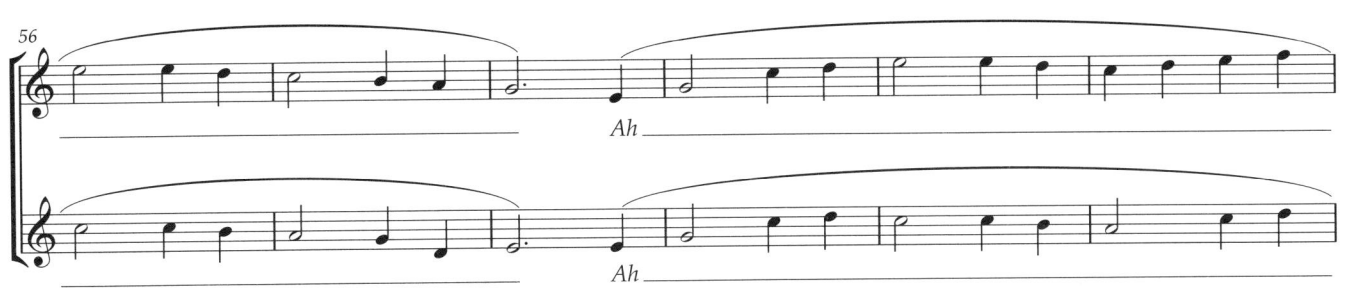

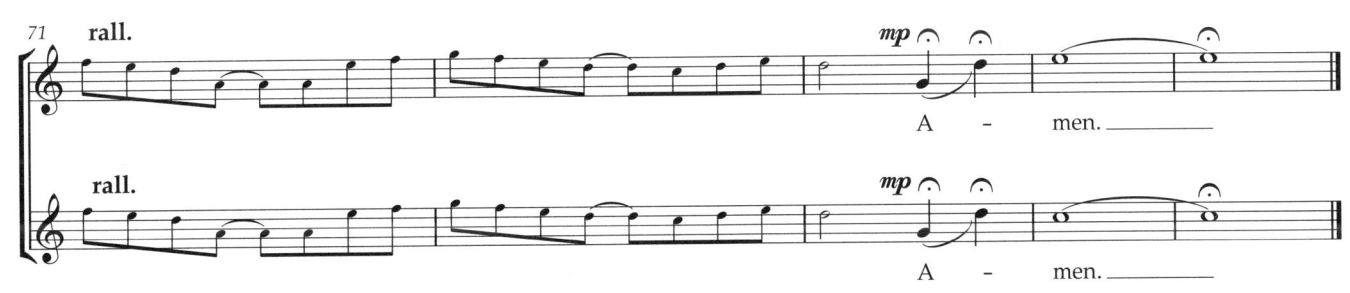

To the choir of West House School, Birmingham

23. God the Singer

Words: Peter Davison

Music: David Ogden

Flowing and strong ♩ = 120

light has re-turned as it came once be-fore, the

song of the Lord is our own song once more;

so let us sing with one heart and one voice the

breath, be glo - ry for e - ver, through life and through death.

ff

Ah

ff

Ah

Ah

Ah

So let us sing with one heart and one voice the Song of the Sing - er in whom we re - joice. A - men.

24. A song of peace and joy

Information

The composer of this piece, Colin Mawby (b.1936), spent his formative years at Westminster Cathedral Choir School in London. He has written many pieces for choir as well as much organ music. Mawby's setting of Psalm 23 became extremely popular since its inclusion on Charlotte Church's *Voice of an Angel* debut album. *A song of peace and joy* is a newly written song, commissioned for the *Voice for Life Songbook*.

Preparation

Ask your singers to look at the first phrase (bars 9–12) and compare this with bars 27–30. Can they spot the similarity in the melodic shapes, and also the rhythmic differences? Likewise ask them to compare bars 13–16 with bars 31–34.

Teaching the song

Start with the opening verse (which is in unison throughout) from bars 9–20. You can either demonstrate this to your singers in two-bar phrases for them to sing back, or you may like to ask your singers to sightread the melody which is based either on arpeggio patterns or stepwise movement.

When you go on to cover the next verse from bar 27, remind your singers of the differences in rhythm they spotted during your preparation time. They will need to be especially careful not to sing through the rests at the beginning of bars 27, 31 and 34. If they find this difficult, allow them to put in a sniff (or a clap) in rehearsal on the rests until they are confident with the rhythm. Make sure this doesn't become a habit though – they need to remove the sniff (or clap) just to imagine it in their heads in performance.

Now teach the final section, covering the upper vocal part first then adding in the lower part. The harmony part is very simple, always moving either exactly in step with the upper part (so the melodic pattern is familiar) or moving by step. The entry notes at the start of each phrase often tend to be in unison with the upper part.

See if your singers can achieve a dance-like feel to this song keeping the crotchet-quaver patterns light and not singing too legato (except where the composer has marked in slurs such as bars 17 and 18).

The melody instrument part could be played on any C instrument, such as flute, violin, oboe, or descant recorder. It is also in the correct range to be played on the treble recorder. Be aware that if you ask a pupil to play this on the descant recorder, depending on their level of experience they may not have covered certain fingerings required to play the whole melody (e.g. the high B flat in bar 34).

Using the voice well

There are many words at the end of phrases in this song that end with sibilant 's' or 'c' sounds. Your singers will need to watch you conducting very carefully at the end of phrases in particular, as well as count and listen to each other to make sure that the ends of such words are precisely together.

Musical skills and understanding

In bar 47 is the marking *mp sub* (short for *mp subito*). What does this mean? (Hint: the dynamic just before is *ff*)

24. A song of peace and joy

Music: Colin Mawby

Sing to the Lord ___ new songs, songs of peace and love, ___

songs of joy, songs of hope, songs of joy ___ and hope, ___

songs, ___ songs, ___ songs of peace, songs of love.

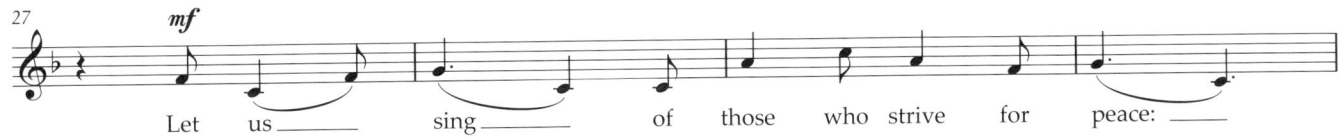

Let us ___ sing ___ of those who strive for peace: ___

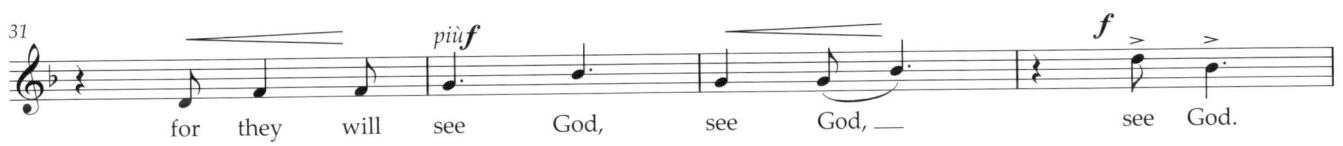

for they will see God, see God, ___ see God.

Let our songs praise, _____ praise those who work for peace.

Let our songs praise, _____ praise those who work for peace.

Let us sing and

Let us sing and

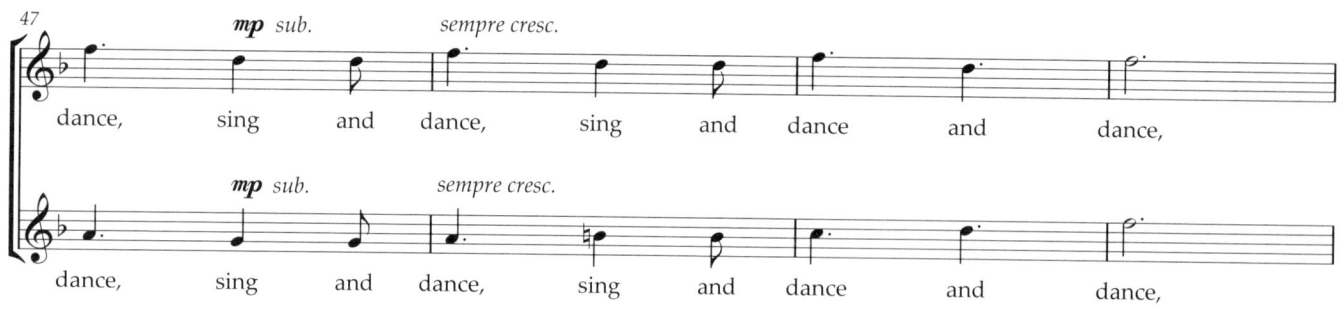

dance, sing and dance, sing and dance and dance,

dance, sing and dance, sing and dance and dance,

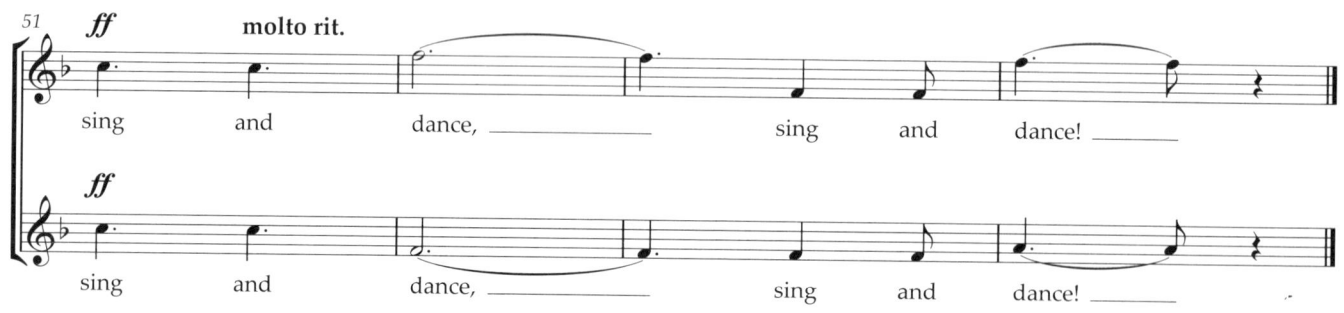

sing and dance, _____ sing and dance! _____

sing and dance, _____ sing and dance! _____

OPTIONAL
INSTRUMENT
in C

24. A song of peace and joy

Music: Colin Mawby

24. A song of peace and joy

Music: Colin Mawby

Sing to the Lord___ new songs, songs of peace and love,___

songs of joy, songs of hope, songs of joy____ and hope, ____

songs, ____ songs, ____ songs of peace, songs of love.

Let us ____ sing ____ of those who strive for peace: ____

for they will see God, see God,___ see God.

OPTIONAL DESCANT

Let our songs praise,___ praise those who work for peace.

Let our songs praise,___ praise those who work for peace.

Two parts and more

25. He came singing love

⊙ **Track 25**

Information

The composer of 'He came singing love' is Colin Gibson, a teacher and writer who lives in New Zealand. Using song as a metaphor for life, the text of this piece suggests that each of us can help love, faith, hope and peace to flourish in our world through living them out in our lives.

Preparation

The melody of this song is based around the tonic chord of E flat. You could start by singing the following pattern to warm-up the voices and get your singers used to the sound and feel of the arpeggio on which the melody is based:

Ah

On each repeat move the exercise up by a semitone. Make sure that the first note is resonant and has plenty of tone.

Teaching the song

Begin by teaching the melody, which is the same for each verse. You can do this by rote, teaching two bars at a time and asking your singers to imitate you (as you would in a call and response song). Alternatively you may like to ask your singers to sightread this melody.

The harmony parts are optional but if you want to perform this song in unison you will need to be aware that the melody is shared between the voices in this arrangement: in the second verse the upper part has the melody, in the third the lower part has the tune, and in fourth verse the melody swaps between the two. Most of the harmonies are fairly simple and memorable, but you could teach sections at a time by making a simple exercise out of the sequences, for example the descant bars 31–32, or bars 42–43 could both be turned into longer descending sequences to get your singers used to the shape of the melodies here.

Using the voice well

Your singers will need good breath control for the diminuendo at the pause in bar 8 if both the tone and pitch are to remain steady. To practise this, ask them to try a gradual crescendo and diminuendo on a single note lower in the register (choose any vowel sound, e.g. 'Ah'). When they can control this change in dynamic, raise the pitch gradually until they can manage this at the same pitch as in bar 8. Once they have achieved this you can add the words back in.

Make sure the up-beat to each verse has a good resonant tone even though it is low for most singers and has a short duration.

25. He came singing love

Music: Colin Gibson
arranged Geoff Weaver

1. He came sing-ing love, and he lived sing-ing love. He died sing-ing

love. He a - rose in si - lence. For the love to go on we must

make it our song: you and I be the sing - ers. _____ 2. He

came sing-ing faith, and he lived sing-ing faith. He died sing - ing faith. He a -

came sing-ing faith, and he lived sing-ing faith. He died sing - ing faith.

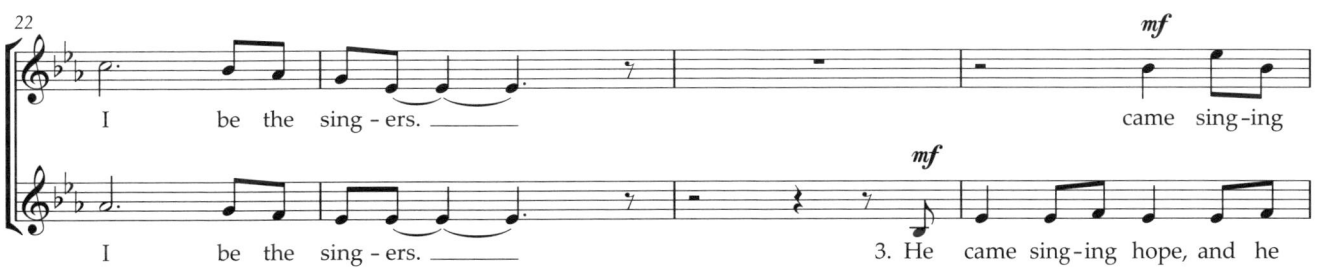

rose in si - lence. For the faith to go on we must make it our song: you and

He a - rose in si - lence. For the faith to go on we must make it our song: you and

I be the sing - ers. _____ came sing-ing

I be the sing - ers. _____ 3. He came sing-ing hope, and he

25. He came singing love

Music: Colin Gibson
arranged Geoff Weaver

1. He came sing-ing love, and he lived sing-ing love. He

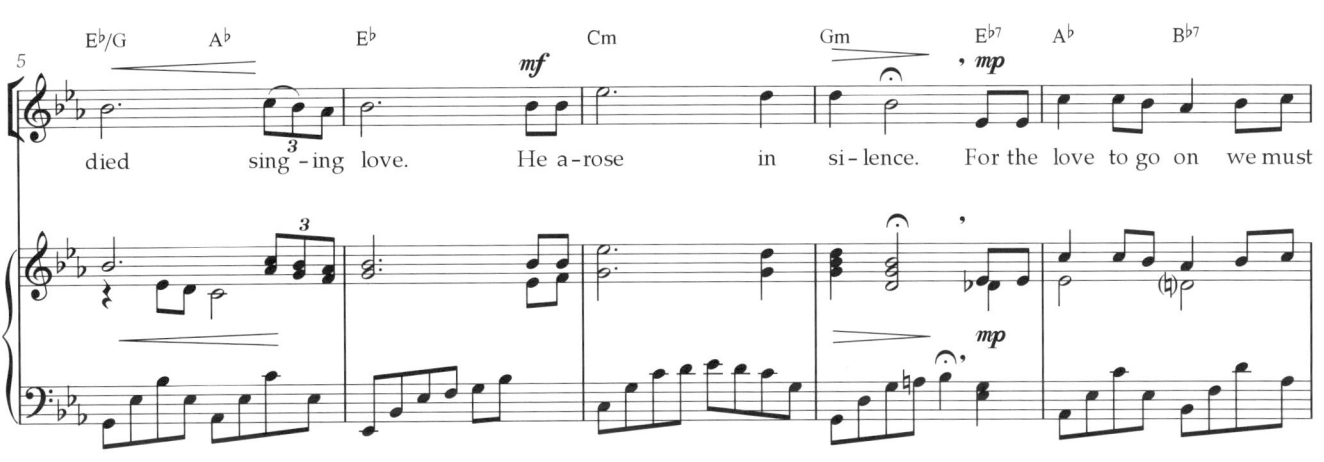

died sing-ing love. He a-rose in si-lence. For the love to go on we must

make it our song: you and I be the sing-ers. _____ 2. He

26

Cm　　　　　　　　Eb/G　　Ab　　　　Eb　　　　　　Cm

hope, lived sing-ing hope, sing - ing hope, he a-rose in __

lived sing-ing hope, he died sing-ing hope, he a-rose in

30

Gm　　　Eb7　Ab　　Bb7　　Gm　　Cm　　Ab　　Bb7

si - lence. Ah _____ ah _____ you and I __ be the

si - lence. For the hope to go on we must make it our song: you and I be the

34

Eb Ab Eb Bb7　Eb Ab Eb Bb7 Eb　　　　　　Cm

sing-ers. _____ 4. He came sing-ing peace, and he lived sing-ing peace. He

sing-ers. _____ 4. He came sing-ing peace, and he lived sing-ing peace. He

117

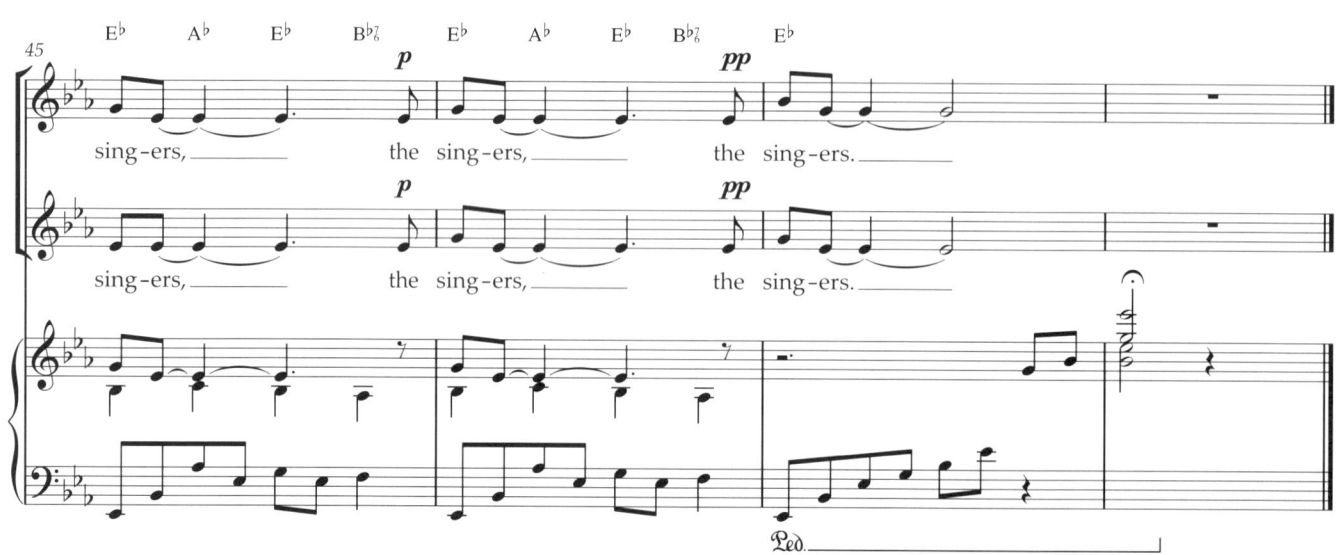

26. Unfinished story

Information

This bright and cheerful song is ideal for use at Christmas and challenges us to consider our response to the birth of Jesus. People all around the world celebrate at Christmas time but not everyone is aware of the origins of the festival or its significance to Christians.

Preparation

To help prepare your singers for the syncopated rhythms in this song, you can introduce them through some clapping games. Ask your singers to walk on the spot (or stamp their feet, if sat down) at a steady pace. Once the pulse is established, clap the following rhythms and ask the choir to clap them back as an echo:

Try making up some rhythms of your own or ask another choir member to take a turn at being the leader.

Teaching the song

It is probably best to teach the melody of this song in four bar phrases. You may need to repeat bars 18–21 ('is what we are hearing but we can determine its end') a few times to enable your singers to get the syncopations and melody correct.

Bars 22–39 are an exact repeat of the melody they have already learnt in verse one, but this time it is shared between the two vocal parts. You will need to split your singers into two teams.

Bars 39–47 (the chorus) is in two parts but both parts are repetitive and simple to learn. Start by asking one team to sing the top part ('Rejoice') over and over again, then while they are still singing this, demonstrate to the other team how their part fits underneath – then get them to try it.

There are one or two moments when the lower part breaks into harmony (e.g. bars 50–53 and 67–70 – the same harmony both times). You may consider this harmony optional, but it is easy to learn as it follows the melody in thirds most of the time.

Using the voice well

See if your singers can roll their 'r's at the beginning of the word 'rejoice' each time – this will give energy and impetus to the start of the note, after which they should allow the sound to diminuendo (but without losing support and with it resonance or pitch). To achieve this effect it may help them to imagine the sound of a bell tolling.

There are a lot of words to fit in, so your singers will need to have energetic mouths, lips and tongues to make sure the text is clear. However, make sure that no tension creeps into the jaw, throat or voice. You might like to take some time out from the song to use some jaw-loosening exercises such as imagining they are chewing on a very sticky toffee, pulling the biggest widest face they can then screwing their faces up really tight or yawning. You could also have a go at a tongue twister!

Musical skills and understanding

The piece begins in F major (B flat in the key signature). What key does the piece modulate to at bar 61 (when there is an F sharp in the key signature)?

How long is the note in the top part in bars 74–75?

What does the performance direction at the beginning of the piece mean (allegro moderato)?

For the choir of Queen Margaret's School, York

26. Unfinished story

Words & music: Philip Godfrey

It was a night in De-cem-ber,

cold De-cem-ber when a light came in-to our world; a light sent from up a-bove us one

night Beth - le-hem be-held. But is that night in De-cem-ber all we re-mem-ber of the

light hea - ven chose to send? An un - fin-ished sto - ry is what we are hear-ing, but

we can de - ter - mine its end.

And he was

we can de - ter - mine its end.

For he was sent to pro-tect us

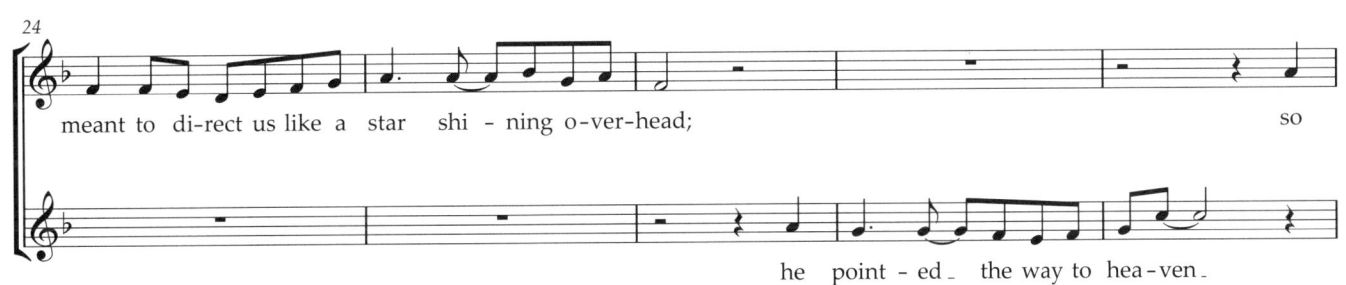

meant to di-rect us like a star shi - ning o-ver-head; so

he point - ed the way to hea-ven.

For the choir of Queen Margaret's School, York

26. Unfinished story

Words & music: Philip Godfrey

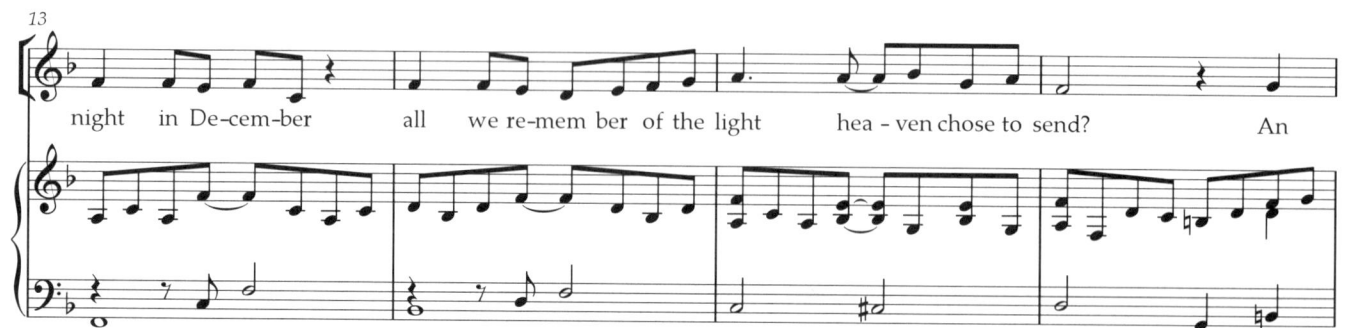

un - fin-ished sto - ry___ is what we are hear - ing, but we can de-ter - mine its

end.

VOICE 1 *mf*
And he was meant to di-rect us like a

VOICE 2 *mf*
For he was sent to pro-tect us

star shi - ning o-ver-head; so

he point - ed___ the way to hea-ven___

clear - ly___ with what he said. But will the world e-ver hear him, ga - ther near him as a

But will the world e-ver hear him, ga - ther near him as a

125

guide, guar-di-an and friend? An un - fin-ished sto - ry_ is

guide, guar-di-an and friend? An un - fin-ished sto - ry_

what we are hear - ing,_ Re - joice!_

but we can de -ter - mine its end. all the an-

_ Re - joice!_ Re - joice!_

- gels _ sang as the church - bells _ rang _ would we hear

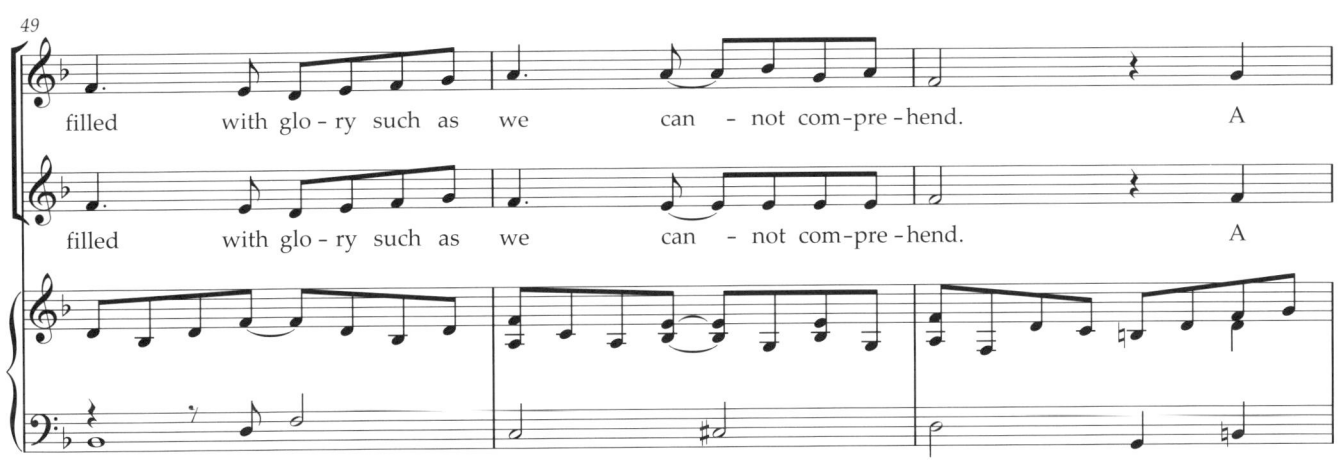

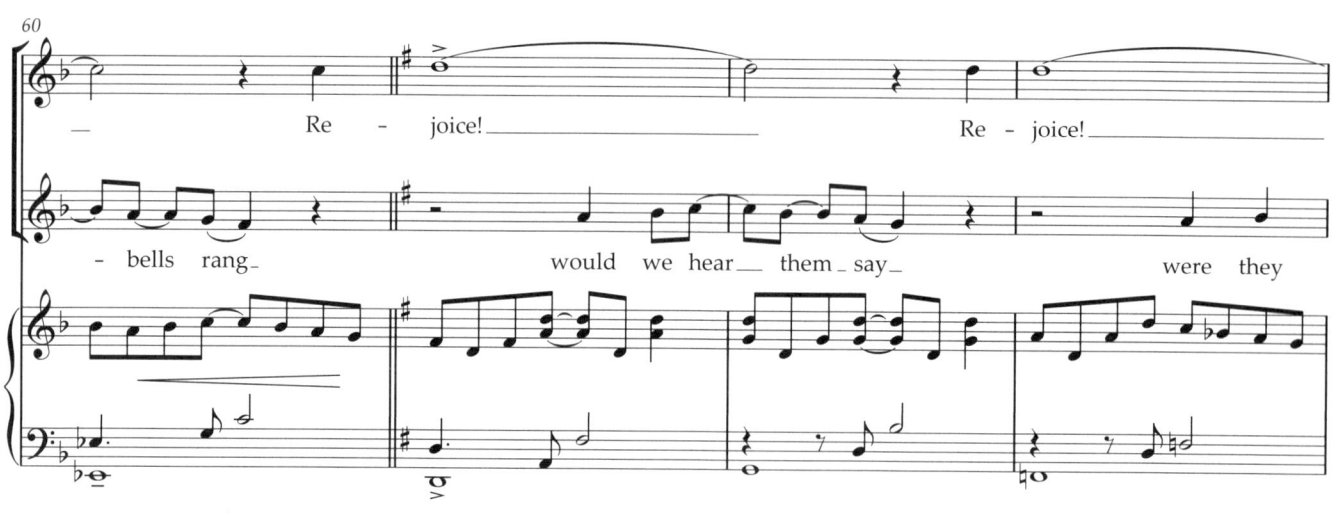

we can - not com-pre-hend. A won - der - ful sto - ry, and

we can - not com-pre-hend. A won - der - ful sto - ry,

(VOICE 1)

we have been gi - ven the chance to com - plete it, a chance that we must not sus -

-pend; Re -

the chance to com - plete it the way we would like it to

-joice! Re - joice! Re - joice!

end. Re - joice! Re - joice!

27. We rejoice to be God's chosen

(•)   **Track 27**

Information

This dance-like song is arranged by John Bell of the Iona Community. The text reminds us that it is by the grace of God that we are chosen to be his people but that this calling is to love, serve and give to others.

Teaching the song

This song is unison throughout with the same melody in each of the verses. Begin by teaching the first four bars of the melody. This is the same as the next phrase and the last phrase in each verse. You may find it helpful to divide the third line into two phrases when introducing it.

The second verse may be sung in unison – in which case you may like to allocate a solo or semi-chorus to sing it. However, some singers may enjoy the challenge of the alternative a cappella version, in which the accompanying parts sing simple, repeated riffs. To teach this, divide your choir into three groups. Introduce the lowest part first, asking the allocated group to repeat it continuously while you demonstrate the upper harmony part at bars 17–20. Next, ask the second group to sing this riff repeatedly. Once these two parts are secure ask the third group to sing the melody over the top. You can then go back and teach your upper harmony part their simple four-bar introduction to this section. You will also need to practise the transition from the first verse to the second to make sure each of the groups can find their starting notes in context.

Practical points

The flute part would also be very effective played on a treble recorder. However, if you do not have a melody instrument available, the piano accompanist can play this melody over the top of their own part.

Be careful not to take the piano introduction too quickly – the melody instrument has a lot of notes to fit in over the top!

Musical skills and understanding

What is the highest note in the vocal melody?

Can your singers describe what the following terms mean: *Maestoso* (bar 33), *ff* (bar 40), *rall* (bar 56)?

What is the duration of the final note?

27. We rejoice to be God's chosen

Nettleton

Words & arrangement: John Bell

-wait where we are sum-moned and ac-cept where we are sent. We re-

-joice to be God's cho-sen and a-midst all that we see, to an-

rall.

-ti-ci-pate with won-der, that the best is yet to be. _____

A CAPPELLA VERSION OF VERSE 2

mp

2. We re-joice to be God's

mp

La la la la la (*simile*)

mp

La la la la la (*simile*)

cho-sen, to be gath-ered to God's side, not to build a pi-ous ghet-to or be

steeped in self-ish pride; but to___ ce-le-brate the good-ness of the___ One who sets us

free from the small-ness of our vi-sion to be-come, not just to be.

27. We rejoice to be God's chosen

Nettleton

Words & arrangement: John Bell

YOU MAY PHOTOCOPY THIS PAGE

27. We rejoice to be God's chosen

Nettleton

Brightly, with a spring ♩ = 105

Words & arrangement: John Bell

mf 1. We re-joice to be God's cho - sen not through vir - tue, work or skill, but be -
mp 2. We re-joice to be God's cho - sen, to be gath - ered to God's side, not to

-cause God's love is gen - 'rous, un - con - formed to hu - man will. And be -
build a pi-ous ghet - to or be steeped in self - ish pride; but to

-cause God's love is rest-less like the_ surg – ing of the sea, we are
ce – le – brate the good-ness of the_ One who sets us free from the

pulled by heav'n's dy – na – mic to be – come, not just to be.
small – ness of our vi – sion to be – come, not just to be.

Maestoso

3. We re – joice to be God's cho – sen, to a – lign with heav'n's in – tent, to a –

-wait where we are sum-moned and ac-cept where we are sent. We re-

-joice to be God's cho - sen and a - midst all that we see, to an - ti - ci - pate with

won - der that the best is yet to be.

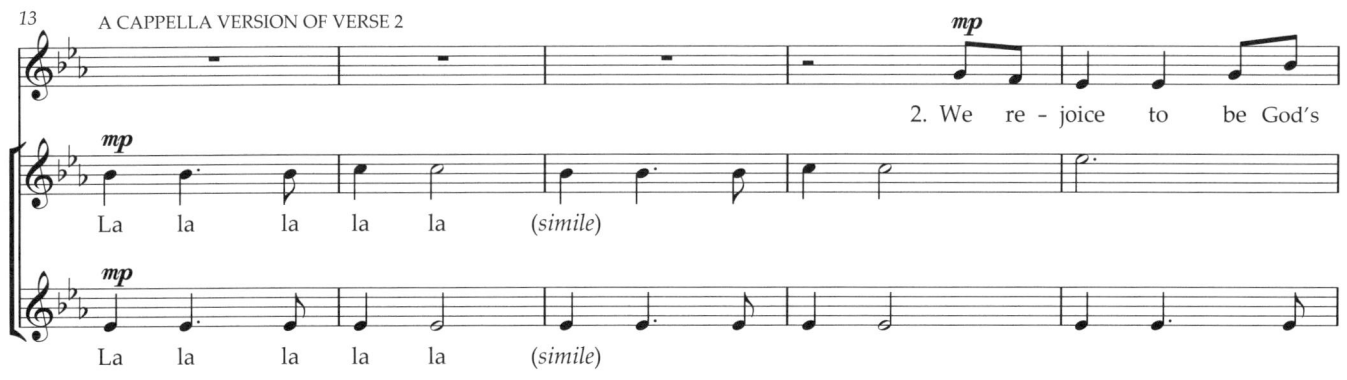

A CAPPELLA VERSION OF VERSE 2

2. We re - joice to be God's

La la la la la (simile)

La la la la la (simile)

cho - sen, to be gath - ered to God's side, not to build a pi - ous ghet - to or be

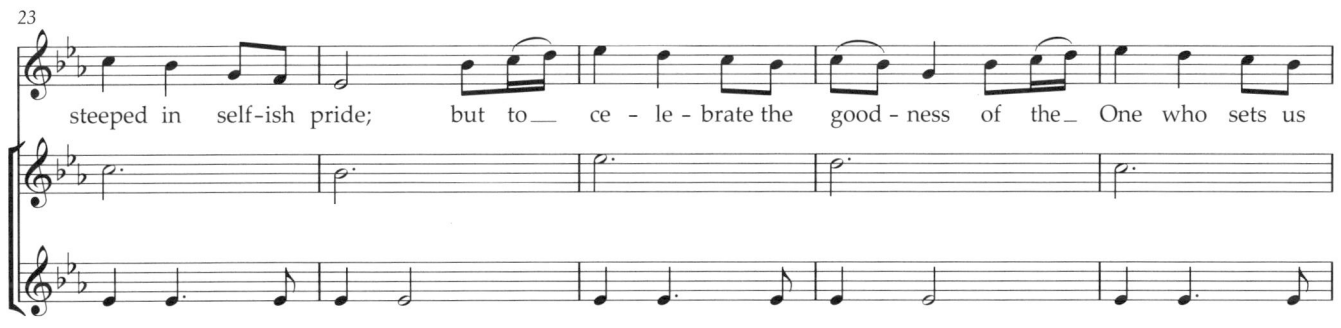

steeped in self-ish pride; but to___ ce - le - brate the good - ness of the___ One who sets us

free from the small - ness of our vi - sion to be - come, not just to be.

28. A prayer of St Richard of Chichester

Information

St Richard (1197–1253) was the Bishop of Chichester for eight years. Richard was elected Bishop by the canons of Chichester when the previous Bishop died in 1244, but King Henry III refused to recognise him as Bishop. For several years, Richard was entirely dependent on the charity and hospitality of the people and clergy, who defied the King. At last in 1247 the King relented.

St Richard is often represented with a chalice at his feet. This is because it is said that once when he was celebrating Mass he dropped the chalice, but miraculously no wine was spilt.

The text of this piece is a prayer which St Richard is thought to have said on his deathbed.

Preparation

Introduce your singers to the descending sevenths which appear in this song by using the interval in a sequence as a warm-up exercise.

First of all ask your singers to try and connect the sound between the notes of the falling seventh by sliding between the notes on the 'ya' sound. When they can do this while keeping the tone even and connected across the interval, omit the slide (they can still 'imagine' it is there). You can then add in the words to this exercise.

Teaching the song

Begin with the melody of verse one. Ensure your singers keep the gradual crescendo going from bar 14 right up to bar 17, aiming for the word 'dear' as the high point of that phrase. Be careful that your singers don't try and rush the last phrase – after the crotchet movement in the previous phrases some of these final notes will feel very long by comparison (especially the four beats notes on 'follow' and 'thee').

You can then go on to teach the harmony part. In bars 49–50 make sure your singers realize that the top part should be singing the same note in both bars here!

Using the voice well

To sustain the legato lines in this piece, decide with your singers where the climax falls in each phrase and where they should breathe (younger singers may need to stagger their breathing if the long lines prove difficult for them). It will be much easier for them to produce a beautiful cantabile line if there is a sense of momentum within each phrase towards a particular point. This will also help communicate the text with emotion.

Musical skills and understanding

The two notes in bars 49–50 in the top part are enharmonically related. Ask your singers to look at these notes, and see if they can work out what the term 'enharmonic' might mean. It may help for them to look at the piano keyboard while they work it out.

What do the following terms mean? *Poco a poco cresc* (bar 14), *poco rit* (bar 50), *a tempo* (bar 51).

In the key signature there are two sharps (F and C): what key is this piece written in?

28. A prayer of St Richard of Chichester

Words: Richard of Chichester

Music: Richard Allain

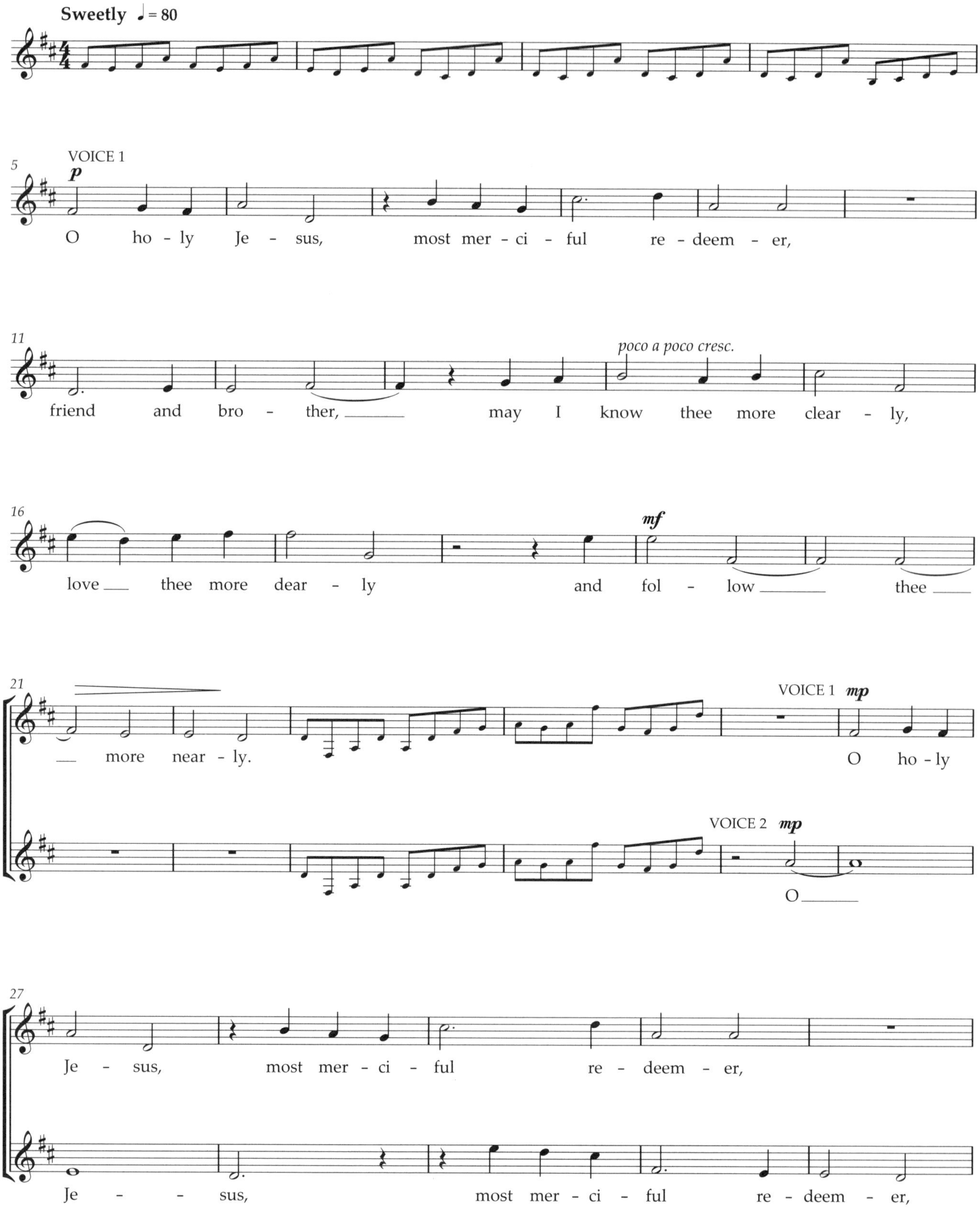

140

friend and bro - ther, _____ may I know thee more

friend and bro - ther, _____ may I _____ know _____

clear - ly, love _____ thee more dear - ly and

thee _____ more _____ clear - ly, _____ love _____ thee more dear - ly

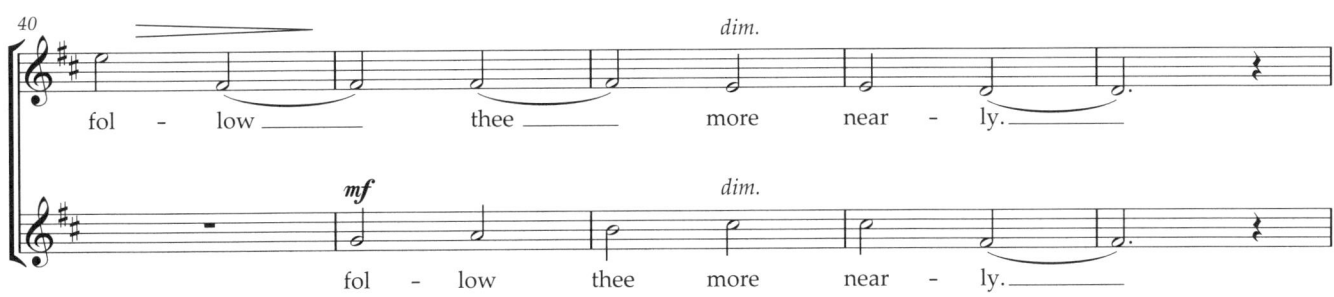

fol - low _____ thee _____ more near - ly.

fol - low thee more near - ly. _____

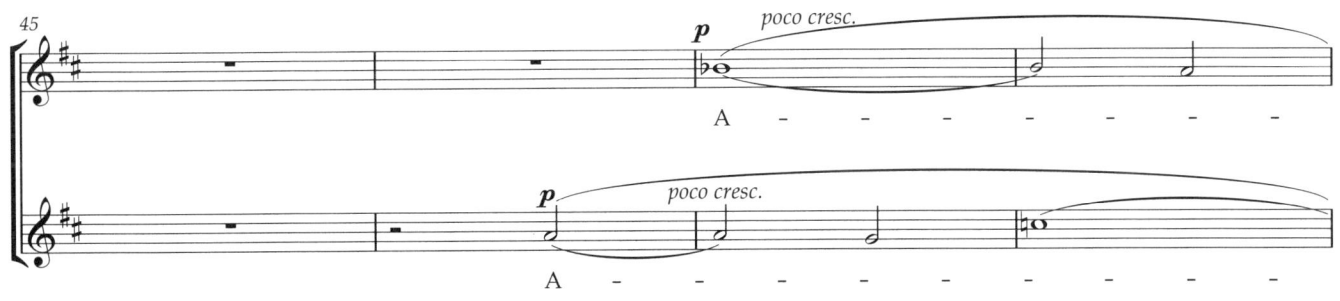

A - - - - - -

A - - - - - - - -

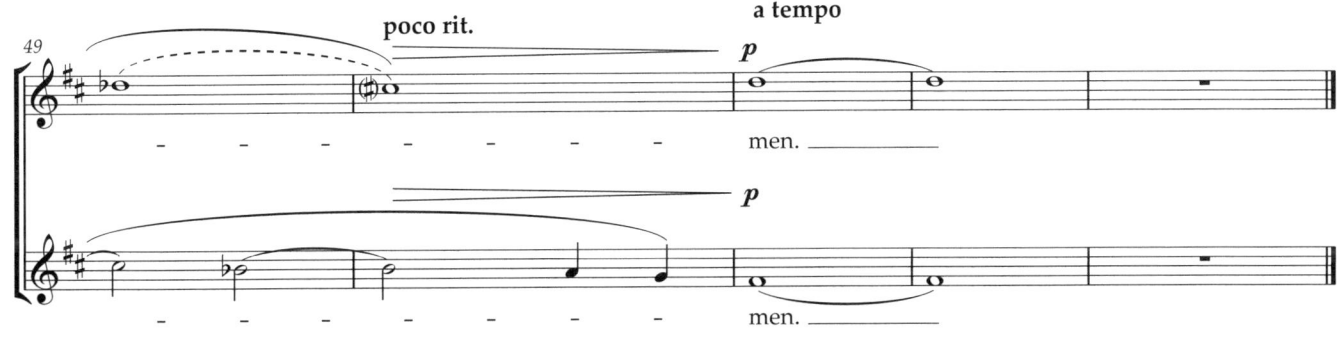

- - - - - - men. _____

- - - - - - men. _____

28. A prayer of St Richard of Chichester

Words: Richard of Chichester

Music: Richard Allain

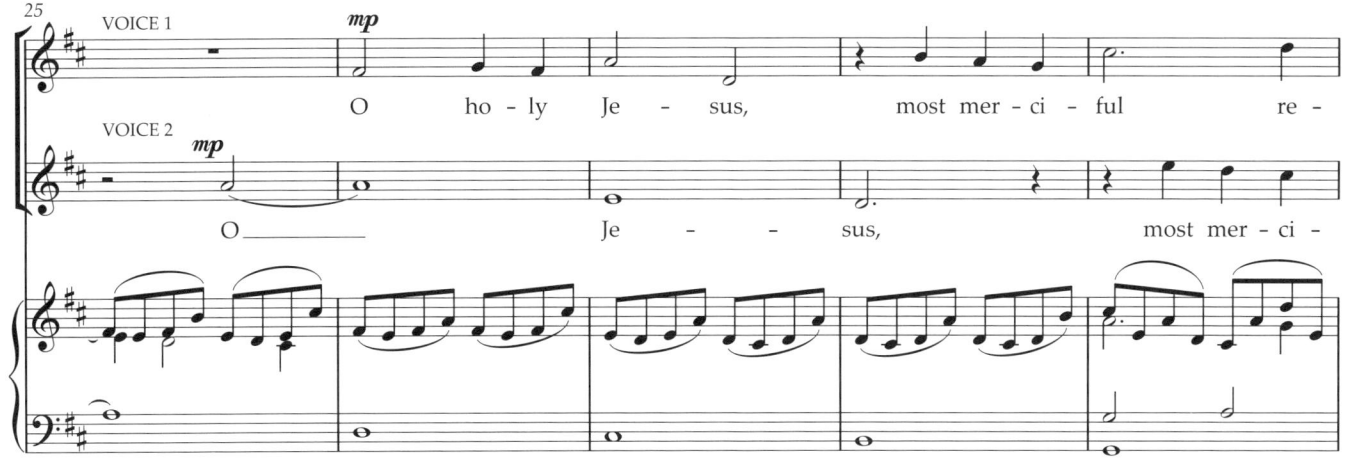

fol - low _____ thee _____ more near - ly. _____

fol - low thee more near - ly. _____

A - - - - - - - -

A - - - - - - - -

- - - - - - men. _____

- - - - - - men. _____

29. For Mary, Mother of our Lord

Information

This song may be used at a service for the Feast of the Annunciation or on Mothering Sunday. The text was written by John Raphael Peacey (1896–1971) who was born in Sussex, England but served as headmaster of a school in Calcutta, India, in the 1930s and remained there through the war years, returning to England in 1945.

Preparation

The first four notes of the melody outline an F major chord. Ask your singers to prepare by singing the following pattern of notes:

Ask your singers to label the notes according to their degree in the F major scale (i.e. 1 3 5 3 1 5 1, where the underscore indicates a low 5). Scramble these numbers into different orders and try singing the new patterns that emerge.

What is the pattern of notes at the start of the melody? Can anyone sightread them without the help of the piano or another singer?

Teaching the song

Start by singing the first verse without the text on an 'ah' vowel: the singers will need to work to maintain a legato line, especially where there are wide leaps in the melody. If possible, they should avoid breathing at bars 8 and 15, preferably by managing two phrases in one breath or by staggering their breathing. Once the tune is familiar, introduce the text.

This melody is repeated in the upper part at bar 21 and then the lower part at bar 56. Work on these sections next, going through the harmony part and the descant respectively and then putting them together with the melody. If this is too demanding for your choir, you could stick to unison at bar 21 and only divide into two parts at bar 56.

Lastly, work on the the middle section of the piece, which begins at bar 38. Make sure that the singers are aware of the dynamic markings. To encourage them to sing piano you could first ask them to hum bars 38–46. When they add the words back in encourage them to retain that small, focused tone but to keep the text loud and energetic.

Using the voice well

When singing quietly some singers will use a breathy tone. This symptom indicates that their breath is not being used very effectively. Most of the time choral singers should aim to maximize their use of air through the use of a focused tone (although there are a few musical styles, such as jazz, that do require breathiness).

The following exercise is helpful to those singers that have trouble producing a focused tone. Ask them to try a nasal laugh, like a witch 'hee, hee, hee' or try an open-mouthed hum on an 'ng' sound opening up onto an 'ee' vowel. Next, they should try singing a few bars of music through on a bright, nasal 'ee' vowel (if they place one finger down the bridge of their nose to feel the vibrations, it may help them focus or 'place' the sound here). When they return to singing normally, with the text, they should try to retain some of this forward placing.

Some singers use this nasal tone all the time when they sing and it is tiring to listen to. They should be encouraged to explore different tonal colours as well.

Musical skills and understanding

The melody of this piece starts with a rising major sixth. Can anyone think of another song that starts with this interval (e.g. *My bonny lies over the ocean*)? On which beat of the bar does the melody start?

In verse two (which starts at bar 21) the harmony part is mainly lower than the melody but crosses it in several places. Can anyone identify where this occurs?

What is the definition of *Andante*?

29. For Mary, Mother of our Lord

Words: J R Peacey

Music: Simon Lole

For Ma - ry, Mo - ther of our Lord, God's

ho - ly name be prais'd; who first the Son of God a -

-dor'd, as on her child she gazed.

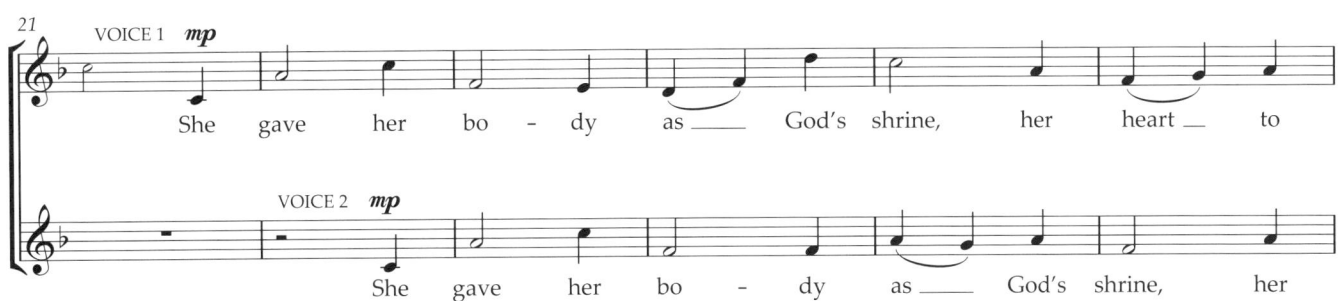

VOICE 1
She gave her bo - dy as God's shrine, her heart to

VOICE 2
She gave her bo - dy as God's shrine, her

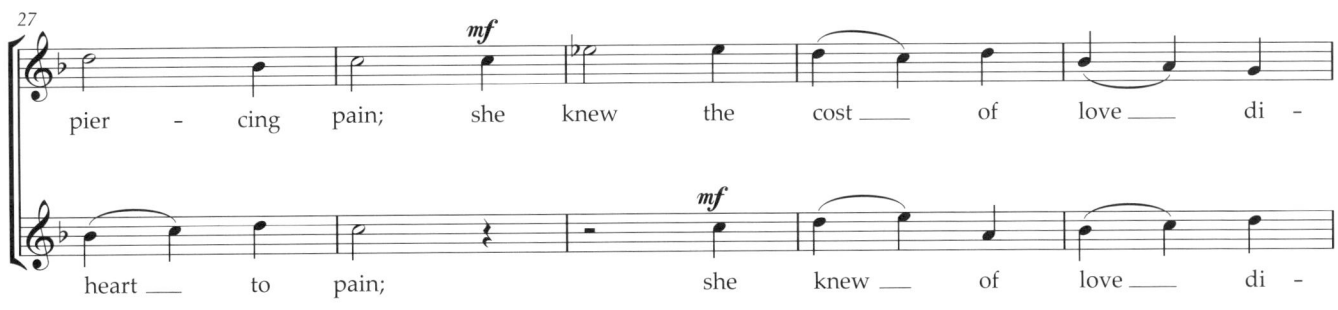

pier - cing pain; she knew the cost of love di -

heart to pain; she knew of love di -

-vine, when Je - sus Christ was slain.

-vine, when Je - sus Christ was slain.

Dear Ma - ry, from your low - li - ness and home __ in

Gal - li - lee, _____ there comes a joy and ho - li -

ness to ev - 'ry fa - mi - ly.

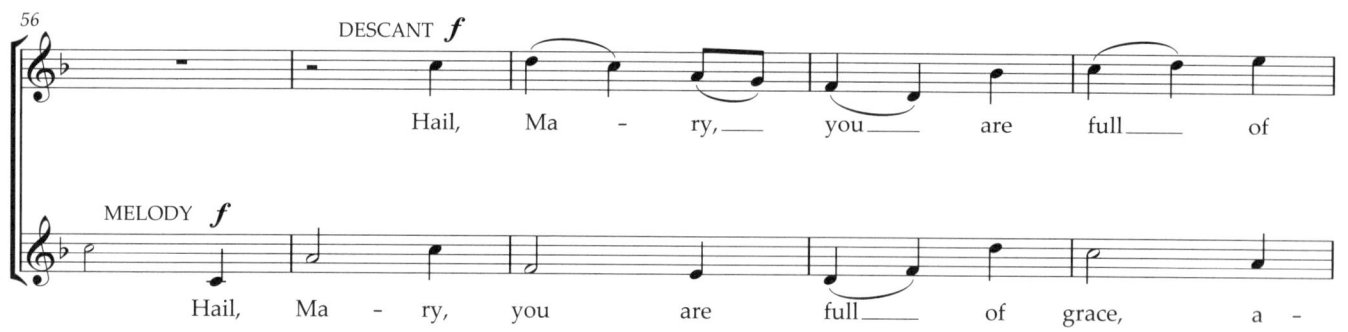

DESCANT *f*

Hail, Ma - ry, __ you __ are full __ of

MELODY *f*

Hail, Ma - ry, you are full __ of grace, a -

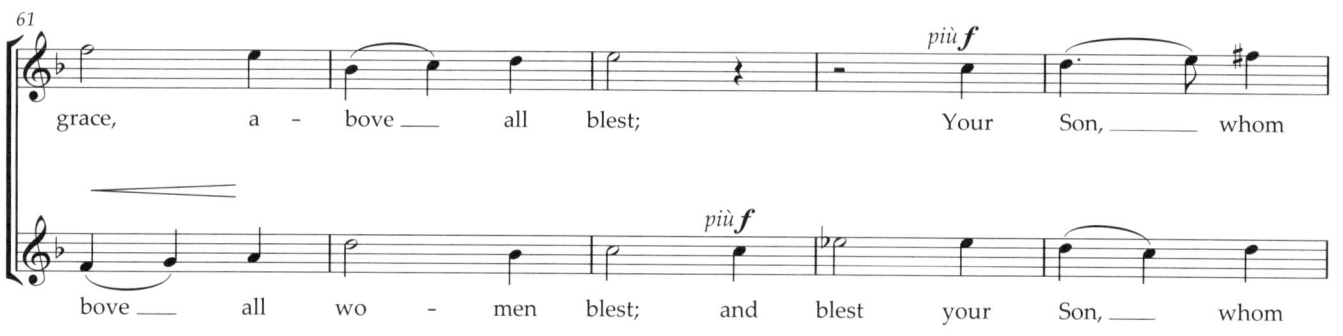

grace, a - bove __ all blest; Your Son, _____ whom

bove __ all wo - men blest; and blest your Son, __ whom

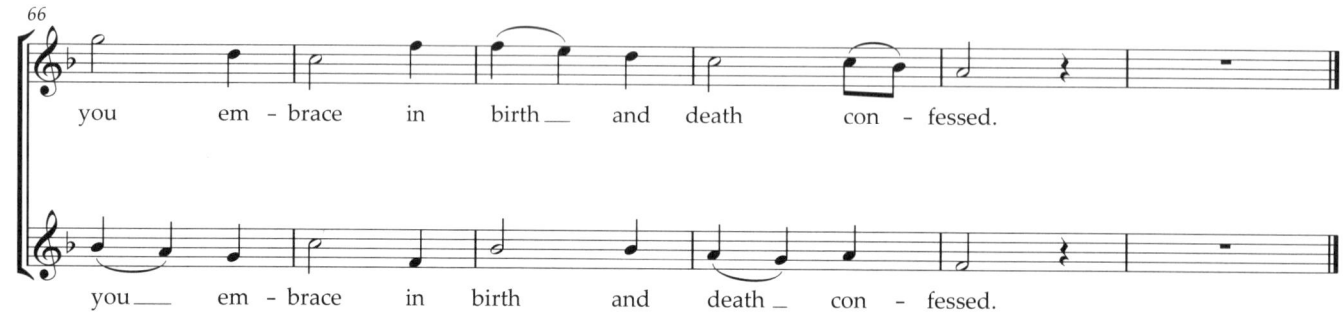

you em - brace in birth __ and death con - fessed.

you __ em - brace in birth and death __ con - fessed.

29. For Mary, Mother of our Lord

Words: J R Peacey

Music: Simon Lole

She gave her bo - dy as God's shrine, her heart to

She gave her bo - dy as God's shrine, her

pier - cing pain; she knew the cost of love di -

heart to pain; she knew of love di -

vine, when Je - sus Christ was slain.

vine, when Je - sus Christ was slain.

UNISON *p*

Dear Ma - ry, from your low - li - ness and home __ in

mf

Gal - li - lee, _____ there comes a joy and ho - li -

- ness to ev - 'ry fa - mi - ly.

30. You're my friend

Information

This song is about friendship and the value of having people we can trust to be there for us, in good times and in bad. There is a challenge here: if we appreciate those around us who offer us that kind of friendship, we, in turn, should be prepared to love and support others in the same way.

Teaching the song

Start with the chorus in bar 12 'When I talk to you, you listen' up to bar 20, teaching in two bar phrases (if teaching by rote). Once the chorus is familiar, go back to the beginning to learn the melody of the verse.

The lower part is optional, so you can perform this song in unison if you wish. If you are including the lower harmony, begin by teaching the section from bar 23 to 39. When the lower part breaks off into harmony from bar 26, it is largely in thirds below the melody and should be a familiar 'shape' for your singers to hear and sing confidently. Make sure your singers are aware when they should be singing in unison though (e.g. the last note of the chorus in bar 39), so that they tune their notes together carefully with the melody.

Next teach the final section from bar 50 to the end. In this section the singers on the lower part can imagine they are 'backing singers' adding in little repetitive harmonies here.

Finally, go back and add in the lower part from bars 43–50.

Using the voice well

Even though there are a number of rests in the chorus section ('When I talk to you, you listen….') ask your singers to think in two-bar phrases and not to breathe at every rest. This will provide a sense of line through the phrases and prevent any of the notes sounding clipped.

Musical skills and understanding

What does *mf* (bar 12) mean?

How many beats should the last note in the vocal parts last?

What does *poco rit. al fine* (bar 60) mean?

What is the difference between the key of the verses and the chorus? How does this change reflect the words of the song?

30. You're my friend

Words & music: Anthony Marks

30. You're my friend

Words & music: Anthony Marks

28

know there's some-where you can go, there's some-one you can call, to catch you if you

know there's some-where you can go, there's some-one you can call, to catch you if you

31

mf

fall. If you talk to me, I'll list - en, ___ If you

mf

fall. If you talk to me, I'll list - en, ___ If you

34

call my name, I'll be there, I'm your friend, I un - der -

call my name, I'll be there, ___ I'm your friend, I un - der -

37

- stand you, I'm your friend, you know I care.

- stand you, I'm your friend, you know I care.

31. May the road rise to meet you

Information

This beautiful song is a setting of a traditional Gaelic blessing. Although it may be used at any time of year, it is particularly suitable for use at weddings or at the end of a church service or concert programme.

Teaching the song

To begin with you can either teach the melody by rote in four-bar phrases, or ask your singers to sightread the first verse of the melody. The harmony part is optional, but if you opt to sing the whole piece in unison think creatively about how you can still achieve contrast and musical interest: you could, for example ask a soloist to sing the melody the first time it appears (bars 8–21), use a small group for bars 28–37 and reserve tutti for the final rendition of the melody.

Although there is only one harmony part, during the second verse this harmony often lies underneath the melody (and would probably be more suitable for singers with lower voices), whereas in the final verse the harmony part is a descant. You may like to use different groups of singers to sing these sections.

Using the voice well

Encourage your singers to use a full dynamic range – the vocal parts cover everything from piano to forte and including these dynamics will significantly improve your performance of the song.

It can be difficult to crescendo without pushing the pitch sharp and to diminuendo without allowing the pitch to flatten, particularly when holding a long note at the end of a phrase (e.g. bars 57–58). You can help your singers practise this by using the following game: ask them to hold a long note to a vowel of your choosing (they should stagger their breathing when necessary). They watch you for the relevant hand signals to crescendo or diminuendo – you can make these long gradual changes in dynamic or rapid changes. All the time they need to concentrate on keeping the pitch absolutely steady.

Musical skills and understanding

The piece starts in B flat major. In what key does it end (from bar 45–end)?

How long does the note on the word 'meet' (bar 17) last?

What does the abbreviation *cresc.* (bar 51) stand for, and what does it mean?

What is the pitch of the highest note in the harmony part (bar 55)?

For Tessa Forbes and Rydes Hill School in the year of its Diamond Jubilee

31. May the road rise to meet you

Words: Traditional

Music: Alexander L'Estrange and Joanna Forbes

Gently lilting; simple and expressive ♩ = 86

(OPTIONAL SOLO OR SMALL GROUP)

mp

May the road rise to meet you, — may the wind be al-ways on your

back. May the sun shine warm up-on your face, the rain fall soft up-on your fields, and un

p cresc.

-til we meet a-gain may — God hold you in the palm of his

hand.

MELODY

mf

May the road rise to meet you, — may the wind be al-ways on your

OPTIONAL HARMONY

mf

May the road rise to meet you, — may the wind be al-ways on your

p cresc.

back. May the sun shine warm up-on your face, the rain fall soft up-on your fields, and un-

mf

p cresc.

back. May the sun shine warm up-on your face, the rain fall soft up-on your fields, and un-

mf

til we meet a - gain may God hold you in the palm of his hand.

til we meet a - gain may God hold you in the palm of his hand.

mf

DESCANT *f*

Ah _____ ah _____

MELODY *f*

May the road rise to meet you, may the wind be al - ways on your

cresc.

_____ ah _____ ah _____ Un-

p cresc.

back. May the sun shine warm up-on your face, the rain fall soft up-on your fields, And un-

cresc.

- til we meet a - gain _____ may God hold you in the

cresc.

- til we meet a - gain may _____ God hold you in the

palm of his hand. _____

palm of his hand. _____

mp espress.

Ooh _____

mp espress. (OPTIONAL SOLO OR SMALL GROUP) *mp*

Ooh _____ May God hold you in the palm of his hand.

FLUTE
(OPTIONAL)

31. May the road rise to meet you

For Tessa Forbes and Rydes Hill School in the year of its Diamond Jubilee

Words: Traditional

Music: Alexander L'Estrange and Joanna Forbes

YOU MAY PHOTOCOPY THIS PAGE

For Tessa Forbes and Rydes Hill School in the year of its Diamond Jubilee

31. May the road rise to meet you

Words: Traditional

Music: Alexander L'Estrange and Joanna Forbes

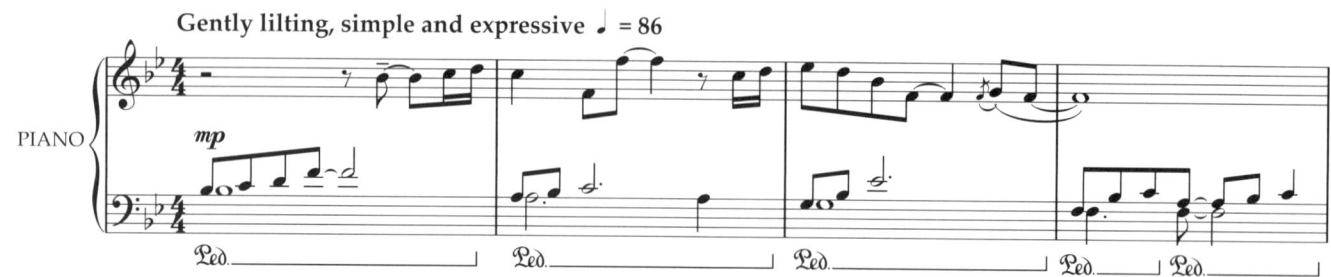

PIANO

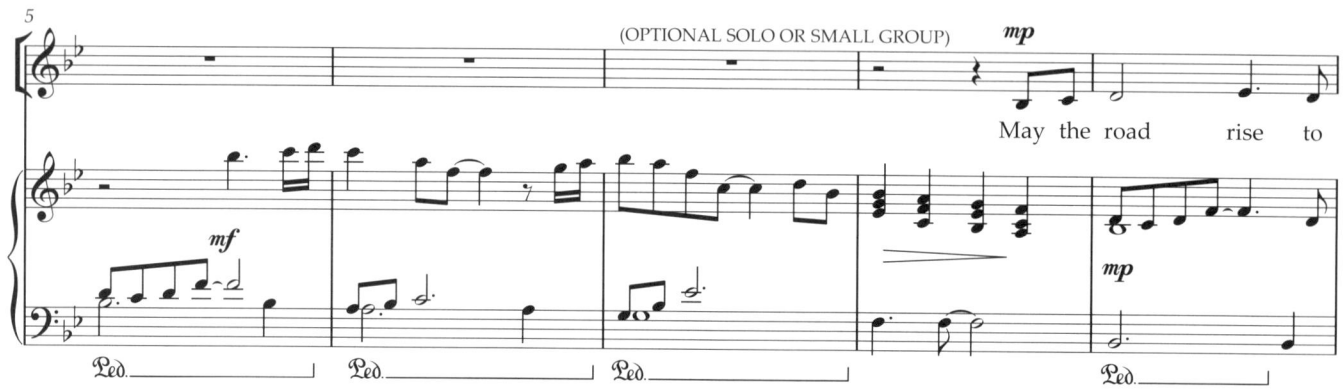

God hold you in the palm of his hand.

MELODY

May the road rise to meet you, _____ may the

OPTIONAL HARMONY

May the road rise to meet you, _____ may the

wind be al-ways on your back. May the sun shine warm up -

wind be al-ways on your back. May the sun shine warm up -

on your face, the rain fall soft up-on your fields, and un-til we meet a-gain may

on your face, the rain fall soft up - on your fields, and un-til we meet a-gain may

God hold you in the palm of his hand.

God hold you in the palm of his hand.

Ooh _____

Ooh _____

(OPTIONAL SOLO OR SMALL GROUP)

May God hold you in the palm of his hand.

poco rit.

poco meno mosso

a tempo

molto rall.

32. Give me strength

Information

The words of this song were written by Black Elk (1863–1950), a Sioux Indian who was a famous holy man (or medicine man). Although he later became a Catholic, he continued to serve as a spiritual leader in his community, seeing no contradiction between what he found valid in both his tribal traditions and Christianity.

Teaching the song

You can either teach the melody by rote in two bar phrases, or ask your singers to sightread the melody. Once you have covered the melody from the beginning to bar 26 teach the harmony part which appears in bars 22–23 (Voice 1). This same harmony appears in bars 47–48.

You might like to jump to work on the last six bars of the piece with your singers next – don't feel you must always begin a song at the beginning and cover the ending last. It can keep your rehearsals interesting and your singers focused if you approach your teaching of songs in a different way.

Finally teach your singers the harmony in Voice 1 from bars 36 to 42.

Musical skills and understanding

This piece is written in C sharp minor. What is the relative major of this key? How do you work out the relative major for a particular key?

What does *pp* (bar 36) mean?

What does *rit.* (bar 56) mean?

What is 'an accidental'? Ask your singers if they can find one in the piece.

For City of Birmingham Young Voices, with David Lawrence,
and Birmingham Festival Choral Society, with Jeremy Patterson

32. Give me strength

Words: Sioux traditional

Music: Bob Chilcott

With a steady beat ♩ = c.80

Give me the strength to walk the soft earth. Give me the eyes to

see and the strength to un-der-stand, that I might be like you.

Give me the strength to walk the soft earth. Give

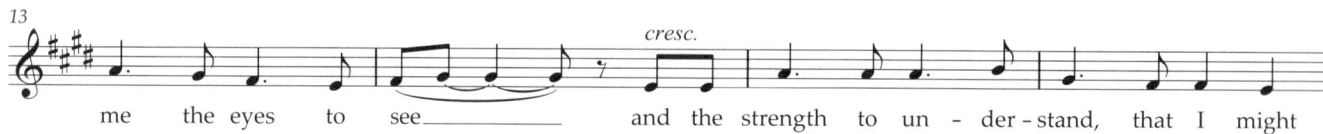

me the eyes to see and the strength to un-der-stand, that I might

be like you. With your power on-ly can I face the winds. All o-ver the earth we

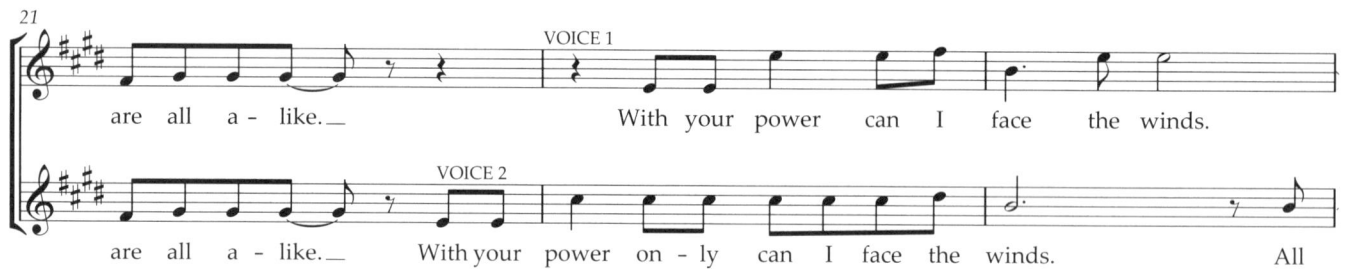

VOICE 1

are all a-like. With your power can I face the winds.

VOICE 2

are all a-like. With your power on-ly can I face the winds. All

VOICE 2

TUTTI VOICES

o-ver the earth we are all a-like. Look up-

For City of Birmingham Young Voices, with David Lawrence,
and Birmingham Festival Choral Society, with Jeremy Patterson

32. Give me strength

Words: Sioux traditional

Music: Bob Chilcott

be like you.__ With your power on-ly can I face the winds. All o-ver the earth we

are all a - like. _ With your power can I face the winds. All

VOICE 1

are all a - like. _ With your power on-ly can I face the winds. All

VOICE 2

o -ver the earth we are all a - like. Look up-

VOICE 2   TUTTI VOICES

-on these fa-ces _____ of child - ren with - out num -ber __

and with child - ren in their arms._____ Look up-

Look up - on, up - on these fa - ces_____ of child - ren

-on these_ fa - ces_____ of child - ren with - out

with - out num-ber and with child - ren in their arms._____ With your

num-ber_ and with child - ren in their arms._____ With your

power on - ly can they face the winds and walk the good road_ to the

day__ of quiet. With your power can they face the winds.

VOICE 2
day__ of quiet. With your power on - ly can they face the winds and

VOICE 2
walk the good road to the day of quiet.

mm __

poco rit. a little slower rit.
Give me strength.

33. Give us light

Track 33

Across the Skies
The Lord is my Shepherd
Ching a Ring
Deep Peace.

Information

The words and music of this arrangement were ... r of Music, born in India in 1944. It is a simple song with a c ... ved through the use of repetition in the melody and drones i ...

Preparation

Make sure your singers understand the geograph ... o repeat the same text and music in bars 5–8 rather than sing ... , the text of which also needs repetition when it is sung later ... ther repeats in subsequent verses.

Explain that the marking over bar 57, D.S. al 𝄌, stands for 'Dal segno al coda'. This means the singers need to return to the sign ('segno') at the beginning of the piece and sing it through again: when they reach the coda sign (𝄌) they should jump to the coda section at the end of the score.

Teaching the song

Start by teaching verse one, where the melody is at its simplest (this section is repeated in the final verse). Next teach your singers verse three: ask one group to keep singing the tune while you demonstrate the upper part (from bars 32 to 41); then get them to imitate what they have heard.

Verses two and four share the same music, so finish by teaching your singers how the vocal parts fit together in these sections.

Using the voice well

Be careful that when singing repeated notes your singers don't let the pitch gradually flatten (e.g. bars 21–23). Ask them to visualise the notes coming from a spot in the middle of their forehead area. This should help to keep them bright.

There are a number of occasions when all the voices sing in unison which is harder to get in tune than your singers might expect. Once they have learnt the melody for verse one, ask them to sing it with their eyes closed, listening carefully to everyone around them for the tuning and timing.

Musical skills and understanding

In this piece, the six crotchet beats in each bar are divided into two groups of three: this is known as a compound time signature. This means that the conductor should beat in two. Ask your singers to practise conducting this piece in two while you play the piano part.

What does *D.S.* mean?

What does the 𝄌 sign stand for?

What is a coda?

33. Give us light

Words and music: Charles Vas
arranged Geoff Weaver

33. Give us light

Jyothi dho Prabhu

Words and music: Charles Vas
arranged Geoff Weaver

34. The spirit of the Lord

 Track 34

Information

The text of this song is based on the words of the Old Testament prophet, Isaiah (chapter 61). In his Gospel account, the historian Luke records that Jesus read this text aloud from the scroll in the synagogue and caused outrage among the religious leaders by revealing that this prophecy was fulfilled through his own life and ministry.

Preparation

Bars 4–13 form a refrain which is repeated after each verse. Ask your singers to look through the score to see whether they can identify the places at which it returns. Are there any differences between these sections?

Teaching the song

Start by teaching the melody of the refrain. Then add in the lower part on the repeat from bars 16 to 25. (This same two-part section appears at bars 38–47, and bars 62–71 although it has modulated into a different key for the final statement.)

Next teach your singers the section of new material from bar 50 to 61 ('To set free those that are downtrodden'). Although this is written in two-parts you might like to ask your singers try sightreading this section. Each entry has been carefully written so that the singers can find their notes with ease – the parts either begin each phrase in unison or they begin on the same note as the previous phrase ended on. Much of the movement in both parts is stepwise, making it an ideal section of music to use for beginners sightreading.

Finally teach your singers the section from bar 28 to 37 ('He has sent me to proclaim release'). The opening of this will be familiar from the previous section you have taught them ('To set free'). The final overlapping phrases 'And recovery of sight' are different, so ask your singers to look carefully at their own vocal part and then at the other part and see where they might find the first note for each of these overlapping phrases.

Musical skills and understanding

This piece passes through several different keys. Ask your singers to look at the following sections and name the key: the beginning (one flat in the key signature), from bar 51 to 60 (three flats in the key signature), bar 61-end (one sharp in the key signature).

What does the performance direction at the beginning mean? (*Andante con moto*).

What does *poco rit.* (bar 72) mean?

What does *a tempo* (bar 75) mean?

34. The Spirit of the Lord is upon me

Music: Ronald Corp

34. The Spirit of the Lord is upon me

Music: Ronald Corp

co-ve-ry of sight to the blind. re - co-ve-ry of sight to the

re - co-ve-ry of sight to the blind, to the

blind. The Spi-rit of the Lord is up-on me, be-

blind. The Spi-rit of the Lord is up-

-cause he has a-noint-ed___ me to preach the gos-pel to the poor, to

- on me, be-cause he has a-noint-ed me to preach___ the gos-pel, to

preach_____ the gos-pel to the poor.

preach_ the gos-pel to the poor.

To set free those who are down-trod-den, to set free those who are down-

To set free those who are down-trod-den, to set free those who are down-

-trod-den, to pro-claim the fa-vour-a-ble year of the Lord.

-trod-den, to pro-claim the fa-vour-a-ble

the fa-vour-a-ble year of the Lord.

year of the Lord, the fa-vour-a-ble year of the Lord.

The Spi-rit of the Lord is up-on me, be - cause he has a - noint-ed

The Spi-rit of the Lord is up-on me, be-

me .... to preach the gos-pel to the poor, ... to preach _____ the

cause he has a-noint-ed me to preach ____ the gos - pel, ... to preach ____ the

poco rit.

gos - pel .... to the poor, ... to preach _____ the

gos - pel .... to the poor, ... to preach ____ the

a tempo

gos-pel .... to the poor.

gos-pel .... to the poor.

35. He's got the whole world in his hands

Information

This is an arrangement of the well-known spiritual 'He's got the whole world in his hands' with a twist. During the course of the song your singers will sing the melody in various musical styles: blues, swing and in canon.

Preparation

To prepare your singers for the introduction to this piece, begin with this rhythm game. Divide them into three teams and give them each a number from two to four. While you clap four beats in a bar ask each of your teams to call out their number on the appropriate beat of the bar. Then, introducing one group at a time, ask them to replace the spoken numbers with the following voice parts:

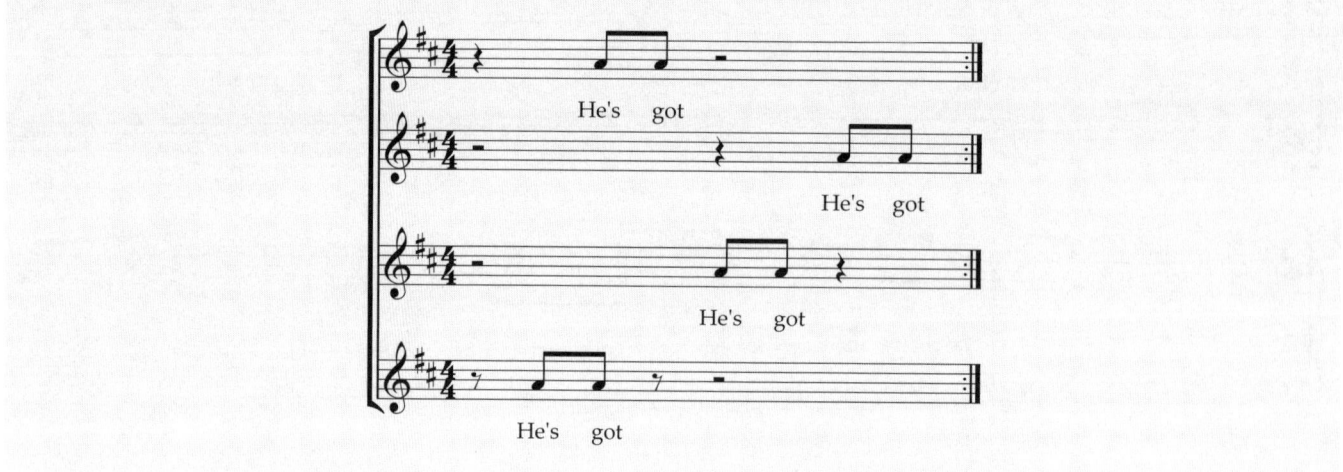

Only add in the syncopated fourth part when the first three parts are secure.

You can then play around, removing some of the parts and leaving others going to see if they can keep the rhythm secure and keep a steady sense of pulse going throughout the game. Set up start and stop signals to encourage your singers to watch the conductor to see when to sing and when to stop.

Teaching the song

Having used the preparation game, look at the introduction with your singers and mark in the beats where each of the 'He's got' entries lies. Then have a go at putting this together.

The melody at bars 17–24 is very much like the original so you could start by singing through this section first. The next section at bars 28–35 is very similar except that the rhythm has been slightly altered so that the fifth note of each phrase is lengthened. Ask your singers to lean on this note to help them remember that they must lengthen it: 'He's got the sun and the moon'. Now divide your singers into two parts so they can sing the melody in canon (bars 37–45).

At this point, go back to the first rendition of the melody during bars 7–13. This is very much like the original melody except that there are a couple of unexpected rests. One comes before the word 'world' and the other before 'in his hands'. If your singers have trouble with this rhythm ask them to imagine doing a 'sniff' to stop them from singing on the rests – 'He's got the (sniff) whole world (sniff sniff) in his hands'. While teaching this section, sing the melody complete and in unison before you break your singers into two parts.

Finally teach the final 'swung' section of the piece, including the harmony underneath.

Using the voice well

During the sections where the melody alternates between the voices, ask the singers to imagine they are singing the whole tune so that they are ready to sing and not surprised each time their entry comes. This should help to keep the melody running smoothly between the parts.

Musical skills and understanding

What key does the music move into at bar 16?

What does *mf* (bar 28) mean?

What does *sempre accel. al fine* (bar 55) mean?

35. He's got the whole world in his hands

Music: Spiritual
arranged Mike Brewer

Fast ♩ = 130

He's got,   he's got,   he's got,   he's got,   he's got the

He's got,   he's got,   he's got,   he's got,

whole world   he's got the   whole world   he's got the   whole world

in his hands,   in his hands,

1.   2.

he's got the whole world   in his hands   he's got the

in his hands, he's got the whole world   in his hands.

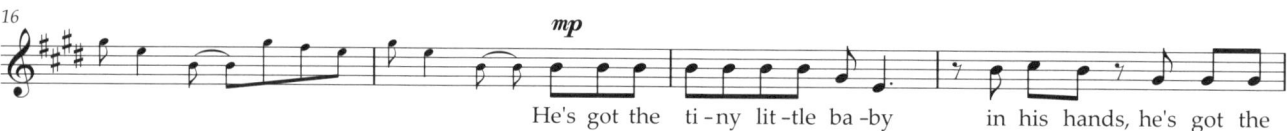

mp

He's got the   ti -ny lit -tle ba -by   in his hands, he's got the

ti - ny lit - tle ba - by   in his hands,   he's got the   ti - ny lit - tle ba - by

2

in his hands,   he's got the   whole world   in his hands.

He's got the sun and the moon in his hands, he's got the sun and the moon

in his hands, he's got the sun and the moon in his hands, he's got the

whole world in his hands. He's got the He's got the

ri-vers and the moun-tains in his hands, he's got the ri-vers and the moun-tains

He's got the ri-vers and the moun-tains in his hands, he's got the

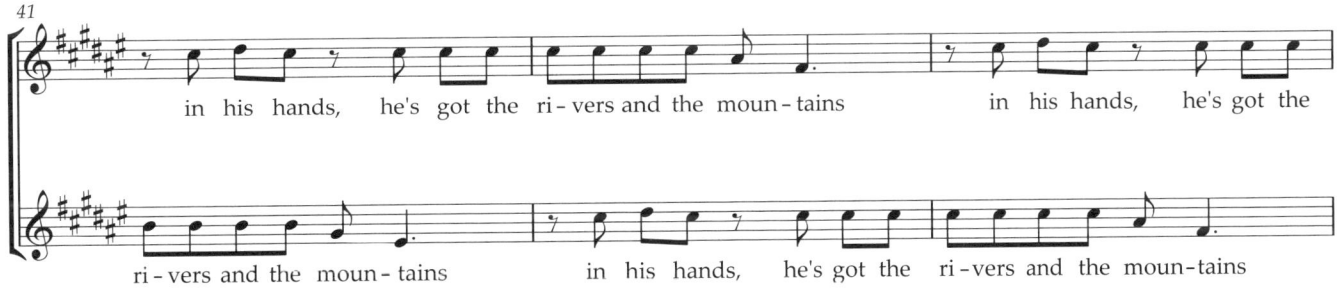

in his hands, he's got the ri-vers and the moun-tains in his hands, he's got the

ri-vers and the moun-tains in his hands, he's got the ri-vers and the moun-tains

whole world in his hands. He's got the

in his hands, he's got the whole world in his hands. whole world in his hands.

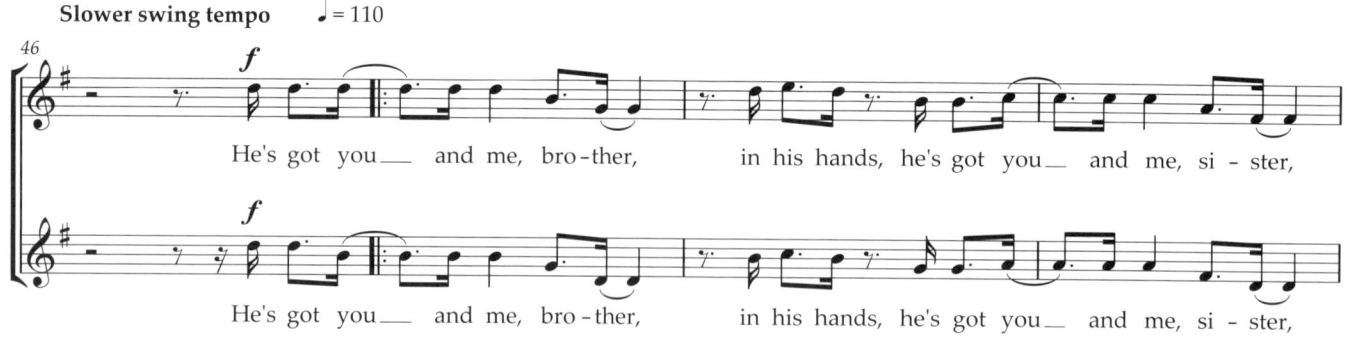

Slower swing tempo ♩ = 110

He's got you___ and me, bro-ther, in his hands, he's got you___ and me, si - ster,

He's got you___ and me, bro-ther, in his hands, he's got you___ and me, si - ster,

in his hands, he's got ev - 'ry-bo-dy here _____ in his hands, he's got the

in his hands, he's got ev - 'ry-bo-dy here _____ in his hands, he's got the

1.

2. *accelerando*

whole world in his hands. He's got the He's got the

whole world in his hands. He's got the He's got the

sempre accel. al fine.

whole world in his hands. He's got the whole world in his hands!

whole world in his hands. He's got the whole world in his hands!

35. He's got the whole world in his hands

Music: Spiritual
arranged Mike Brewer

He's got the

Rock arms

He's got the ti-ny lit-tle ba-by in his hands he's got the ti-ny lit-tle ba-by

in his hands he's got the ti-ny lit-tle ba-by in his hands, he's got the whole world in his hands.

Jazz funk

He's got the sun and the moon in his hands he's got the sun and the moon

in his hands, he's got the whole world in his hands. He's got the

ri-vers and the moun-tains in his hands, he's got the whole world in his hands.

Slower Swing tempo ♩ = 110 *f*

He's got you

whole world in his hands. He's got you

Slower Swing tempo ♩ = 110

and me, bro - ther, in his hands, he's got you and me, si - ster,

and me, bro - ther, in his hands, he's got you and me, si - ster,

36. If there is to be peace

Information

This song is based on a text by Lao Tzu (B.C. 570–490), a sixth-century Chinese philosopher. It is particularly suitable for use at Remembrance, but may also be used for services on the theme of war and peace.

Teaching the song

This short, through-composed piece does not have a chorus or repeating verses. You may like to use it as a sightreading exercise the first time you sing it through. Then, as you break it down into smaller sections to teach the notes, why not start at the end of the song (from bar 30 to the end) which is largely in unison. The end of a song very often gets ignored and is often the part sung (and known) the least, so it can be really useful to sing the end first and keep adding phrases to the beginning of this.

Once you have covered the end of the song, go back and teach the section from bars 23 to 29 (the upper part first, then the lower part). Once this is secure, sing from here right to the end of the piece.

Next teach the section from bar 16 to 21, where the melody line almost alternates between the vocal parts. Encourage your singers to really enjoy the suspension at the beginning of bar 18! Again, having covered this new section sing from here right to the end of the piece so that your singers feel more and more familiar with the music.

Do the same with the section from bar 9 to 13. Make sure the singers on the lower part feel confident about where to find their first notes (e.g. bar 10, where it is the same note as the upper part is singing). If there is nowhere obvious for them to find their first note from (e.g. bar 12), ask the upper part to sing the previous bar and stop on the first beat of bar 12, while you demonstrate the note the lower part should sing. Then do the same but ask your singers of the lower part to join you this time. Continue to do this until they have internalized the sound of that note. Finally go back and teach the opening section from bars 4 to 8.

Using the voice well

There are a number of words ending in either 's' or 'c' in this text. Your singers will need to watch you very carefully so that they all finish the word at the end of each phrase together. It will be especially noticeable if singers are not counting or watching the conductor – even one person placing this 's' sound early (or late) will be heard!

The choir will also need to be very disciplined about their breathing, always going through each three-bar phrase in one breath (i.e. only breathing when they see any punctuation marked in the text.) Any unnecessary 'sneaked' breaths in the middle of a phrase (e.g. after the word 'peace') will be heard as your singers will probably put an early 'c' in order to take their breath.

Musical skills and understanding

At the beginning of bar 18 there is a dissonance (or clash) between the two vocal parts which only resolves as the upper vocal part moves down onto the C on the third beat of the bar. Do any of your singers know what this kind of dissonance is called? (A suspension.)

36. If there is to be peace

Music: Richard Shephard

If there is to be

If there is to be

peace in the world, there must be peace in the na - tions.

peace _ in the world, there must be peace in the na - tions.

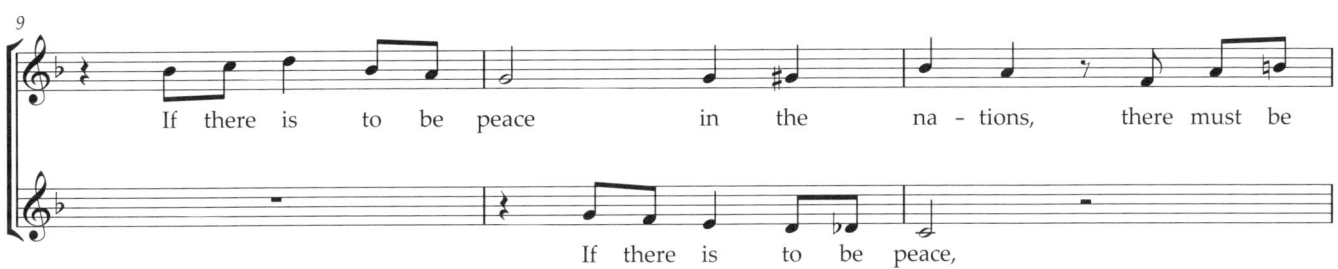

If there is to be peace in the na - tions, there must be

If there is to be peace,

peace in the ci - ties.

peace in the ci - ties.

If there is to be peace in the ci - ties,

If there is to be peace in the

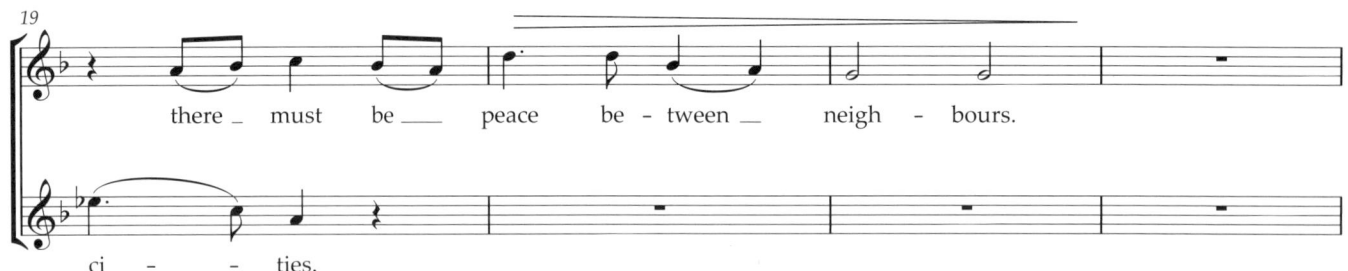

there _ must be _ peace be - tween _ neigh - bours.

ci – – ties.

f

If there is to be peace be - tween _ neigh - bours,

f

If there is to be peace be - tween _ neigh - bours,

sempre *f*

there must be peace _ in the home.

sempre *f*

there must be peace _ in the home.

f

If there is to be peace in the home,

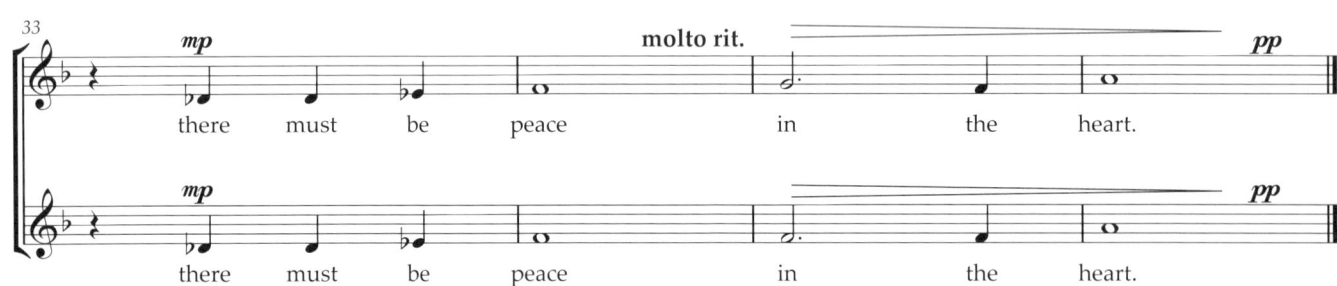

mp **molto rit.** *pp*

there must be peace in the heart.

mp *pp*

there must be peace in the heart.

36. If there is to be peace

Music: Richard Shephard

peace in the ci - ties.

peace in the ci - ties.

mf

If there is to be peace in the ci - ties,

mf

If there is to be peace in the

there must be__ peace be - tween__ neigh - bours.

ci - ties.

If there is to be peace be-tween neigh-bours, there must be peace_ in the

If there is to be peace be-tween neigh-bours, there must be peace_ in the

home. If there is to be peace in the

home.

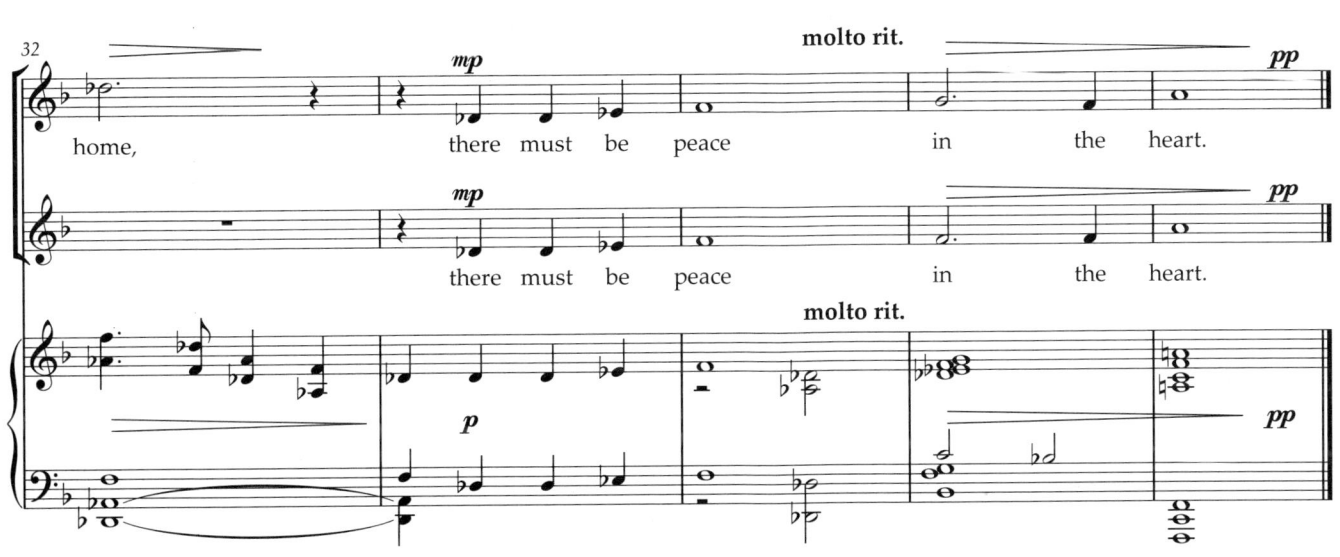

home, there must be peace in the heart.

there must be peace in the heart.

37. This little light of mine

Information

This well-known spiritual was sung at the US Civil Rights rallies in the 1960s. The text speaks of each of us being confident in who we are, and also refers to what Jesus told us 'You are the light of the world…. let your light shine before men that they may see your good deeds and praise your Father in heaven'. We have an example to set to those around us.

This song been arranged and performed by many different people and ensembles over the years. This setting is by American composer and choral conductor, Robert Isaacs.

Preparation

To help your singers with the syncopations, speak the following rhythm as you click your fingers on the beat, then ask your singers to imitate you.

When they are happy with this you can introduce them to other syncopated rhythms in the song by turning this into a call and response game. Keep a regular two-in-a-bar pulse going (either clicking or clapping) and demonstrate a four-bar phrase to your singers for them to copy. If they don't get the rhythm right, repeat it again for them to imitate but don't stop the pulse or the game! When they have one phrase correct move on to a different one. You might like to try and incorporate some of the following phrases from the song:

- This little light of mine, I'm gonna let it shine (bars 17–20)
- Hide it under a bushel, NO!, I'm gonna let it shine (bars 33–36)
- Don't let Satan blow it out, I'm gonna let it shine (bars 65–68)
- Let it shine, let it shine, let it shine (bars 76–80 top part)
- Shine all over your town, I'm gonna let it shine (bars 101–104)
- Let it shine till Jesus comes, let it shine (bars 129–132)

Teaching the song

Although you may chose to perform this piece from memory, your singers will need to learn it from the score. However, you might like to begin work on this song by teaching bars 1–16 by rote to the group singing Voice 2. Ask them to repeat it a few times and then demonstrate the melody from bars 17 to 32 as they sing. Finally, ask the singers of the melody part to imitate you. This opening section is a chorus section that appears several times throughout the song.

Next you should allocate the solo sections of the verses. Don't feel you have to use the same soloists for everything – see how many singers can manage a short line on their own. If you divide the solos between several people, it will reduce the burden of learning. Make sure the choir knows who sings what at bar 107–108 where the music is in four parts.

Every verse is different and the solo sections should have an improvisatory feel. Some of the rhythms are difficult to sightread, but on the first run through encourage your singers to be bold and keep going: you can put it right at a later stage. Even if it all falls apart in the verses, everyone will be able to find their place again at the refrain.

The refrain is repeated twice after the fourth verse with a short coda to finish. Both versions of the refrain are different to the original and will need separate rehearsal. The end needs to be just as confident, rhythmic and exciting as the beginning!

Musical skills and understanding

What is the time signature in this piece? What do the two numbers signify?

This song is written in the key of G major (with one sharp – F). There is one note that doesn't belong in G major which keeps appearing as a 'blue note'. Can your singers tell you which note?

What does *tutti* (bar 34) mean?

37. This little light of mine

Words & music: Spiritual
arranged Robert Isaacs

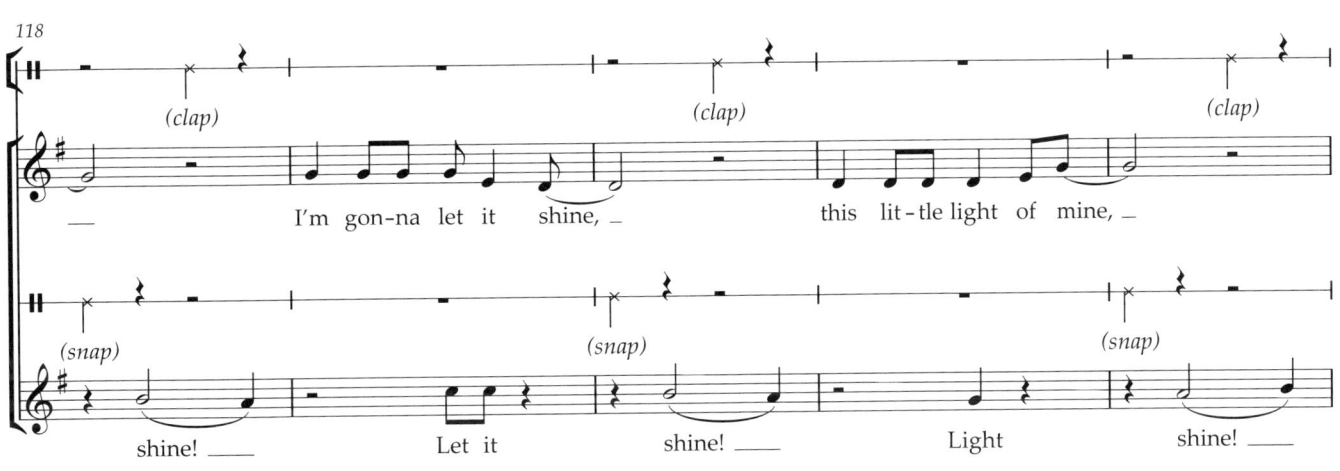

4. Let it shine 'til Je - sus comes, _ let it shine! _ Let it shine 'til

4. Let it shine 'til Je - sus comes, _ let it shine! _ Let it shine 'til

Je - sus comes, _ let it shine! _ Let it shine for Je - sus!

Je - sus, _ Je - sus, _ let it shine! Let it shine for Je - sus!

I'm gon-na let it shine, _ let it shine, let it shine, let it shine! _____

I'm gon-na let it shine, _ shine, shine, shine! _____

This lit - tle light I'm gon-na let it This lit - tle light

Light shine! ___ Let it shine! ___ Light

I'm gon-na let it This lit - tle light

shine! ___ Let it shine! ___ Light shine! ___

cresc.

I'm gon-na let it let it shine, let it shine, let it shine! _____

cresc.

Let it shine, ___ shine, shine, shine! _____

161

This lit-tle light of mine, __ *(clap clap)*

This lit-tle light of mine, __ *(clap clap)* I'm gon-na let it shine,

164

I'm gon-na let it shine, __ *(clap clap)* This lit-tle light of mine, __ *(clap clap)*

(clap clap) This lit-tle light of mine, __ *(clap clap)* I'm gon-na let it shine,

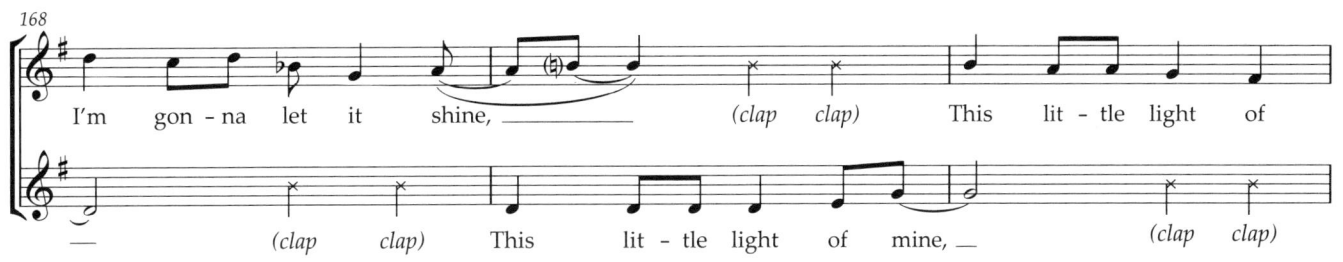

168

I'm gon-na let it shine, _____ *(clap clap)* This lit-tle light of

__ *(clap clap)* This lit-tle light of mine, __ *(clap clap)*

171

mine, _____ Let it shine, Shine! shine, shine,

I'm gon-na let it shine, __ Let it shine, let it shine, shine, let it,

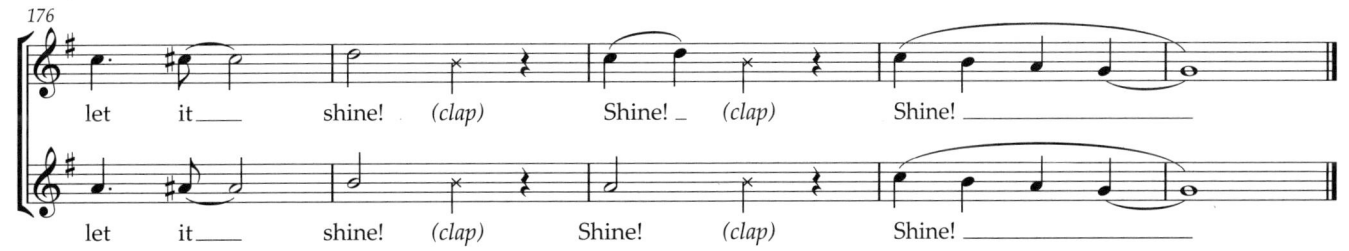

176

let it __ shine! *(clap)* Shine! __ *(clap)* Shine! _____

let it __ shine! *(clap)* Shine! *(clap)* Shine! _____

38. Halle, halle, hallelujah!

⦿   **Track 38**

Information

This short Caribbean song can be used as part of a warm up. The simple countermelodies provide an excellent opportunity for developing part singing. As it comes from the oral tradition it is easy to teach without the music and should ideally be sung from memory in performance.

Preparation

Teach the melody to your choir by rote. If they struggle with the syncopation around the rests you can include a clap during your rehearsal:

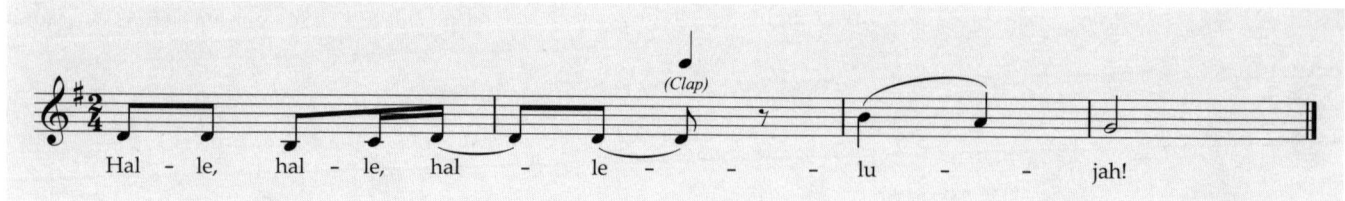

Make sure your singers don't sing through the rests, even when the word itself carries over (as above).

Next teach the countermelodies. The singers of Countermelody 1 need to imagine they are double basses producing the walking bass line – this shouldn't be sung too legato – they should imagine that the strings are being plucked not bowed!

Once all the parts are secure, perform the song through. Be creative about building up the parts, and perhaps even removing a part so that your singers can enjoy hearing how their parts fit together.

Musical skills and understanding

What key is this short song written in?

What is the pitch name of the lowest note in Countermelody 1?

What is a leger line? Where can you find an example in the score?

Can anyone identify the first rest in the melody part (bar 2)? What type of rest is it? How long should it last?

38. Halle, halle, hallelujah!

Music: Traditional Caribbean
arranged Leah Perona-Wright

Hal-le, hal-le, hal - le - lu - jah! Hal-le, hal-le,hal - le - lu - jah!

Hal-le, hal-le, hal - le - lu - jah! Hal-le - lu-jah! Hal - le - lu - jah! _____

COUNTERMELODY 1

Hal - le - lu - jah! Hal - le - lu - jah! Hal - le - lu - jah! Hal - le - lu - jah!

Hal - le - lu - jah! Hal - le - lu - jah! Hal - le, Hal - le - lu - jah!

COUNTERMELODY 2

Hal - le - lu - jah! (clap) Hal - le - lu, hal - le - lu - jah! (clap) Hal - le - lu,

hal - le - lu - jah! (clap) Hal - le - lu, hal - le - lu - jah! (clap) Hal - le - lu - jah! _____

39. I'm gonna sing

Information

This uplifting traditional African-American song can be used in a concert programme, or to celebrate themes of music, worship or obedience to God. You may also like to include it as part of a warm-up.

Teaching the song

Teach this song by rote so that your singers aren't constrained by holding music – then you'll be able to add actions and movement to your performance.

Start by teaching the harmony parts, building up from the lowest part first. (While you are teaching your singers the notes it is probably best to keep repeating the words of the first verse so they can focus on getting the notes and rhythms right.) As one part becomes secure, ask a group of singers to keep singing that part while you demonstrate the next harmony part over the top – the next group of singers can then imitate what they have heard you sing, and so on until you have all the parts being sung together. Then you can sing through the other verses of the song.

Be creative

Don't feel that all the harmony parts must be sung throughout the whole song. Feel free to experiment with introducing the harmony parts and then taking them out for a verse. In particular you may like to introduce the descant only at the end of the song to give the final verse a lift rather than use it all the way through the song.

You may also like to include the optional vocal percussion parts in your performance (or invent your own) along with actions or movement to accompany the verses like 'I'm gonna dance when the Spirit says dance'.

For a fun game in your rehearsal you could ask your singers to think of alternative verses which everybody then sings, (for example 'I'm gonna sit', 'I'm gonna stand', 'I'm gonna bow', 'I'm gonna run', etc) adding the appropriate actions.

Musical skills and understanding

This piece is written in G major (with F sharp in the key signature). Can your singers find any notes in the music which don't belong in this key (e.g. 'accidentals'.)

What is the pitch name of the lowest note in the Harmony 2 part?

What is the pitch name of the highest note in the descant part?

Which of the following Italian terms best describes the mood and tempo of this piece: *Allegro, Adagio* or *Andante*?

39. I'm gonna sing

Words & music: Traditional African-American
arranged Esther Jones

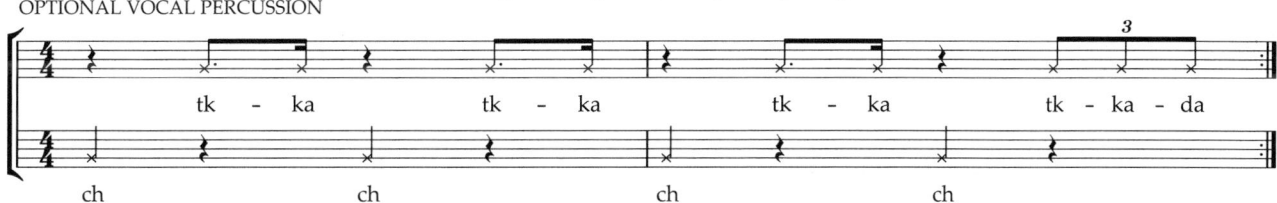

2. I'm gonna shout when the Spirit says shout . . . .

3. I'm gonna pray when the Spirit says pray . . . .

4. I'm gonna dance when the Spirit says dance . . . .

5. I'm gonna sing when the Spirit says sing . . . .

40. Sizohamba naye

Information

This traditional song from Swaziland is about the life of a Christian – to walk through life following the example of Jesus who has gone before us. It fits well at the end of a service and can be sung in procession – although you may find that rather than walking out people may end up dancing!

Preparation

The first verse is in Swazi so have a look through it to make sure you can pronounce it all before you demonstrate to your singers. Don't worry if you are not certain how to pronounce it: an authentic accent is not essential! Before you begin teaching the notes of the song you may want to speak the words 'Sizohamba naye' slowly to your singers and ask them to repeat it back. Once they are happy with the pronunciation start teaching the song.

Teaching the song

Begin by teaching your whole group the melody line with the Swazi text. Then divide your singers into groups and teach Harmony 1 and 2. Finally you can add in the descant. You will need to listen to the balance to work out how many singers you need on each part. The melody needs to be heard at all times so you will probably need the largest group for this (or simply ask the other groups to sing more quietly if they are drowning it out). The descant would work well sung by a soloist.

You will need to decide how you want to begin the piece: you could start with the harmony parts: part 2, then 1, then finally adding the melody over the top, or you may prefer to begin with your whole group singing the melody in unison and then have your singers break off into their harmonies from verse 2 onwards.

Although it is difficult for a non-African choir to precisely imitate the sound of African singers, you should encourage your choir to adopt a robust and hearty sound in keeping with the style. Singers should try to retain some speech quality in the sound and avoid sounding too much like cathedral choristers.

If you can find any recordings (there are many websites that include sound samples of world music for instance), play them to the choir so they get an idea of what they should be aiming for.

Be creative

Traditionally this kind of music would not be sung while the performers stand completely still – singing always comes hand in hand with some kind of movement or dance. Encourage your singers to feel the rhythm by physically moving as they sing.

While you add in the off-beat clicks (or claps) you could ask your singers to walk on the spot in time to your clicks – or alternatively you could get them to walk around the room while they sing.

Musical skills and understanding

What is the pitch name of the highest note in the descant?

Look at the rests in the last bar of Harmony 1 and 2. What kind of rest is this? How many beats is it worth?

40. Sizohamba naye

Music: Traditional Swazi
arranged Leah Perona-Wright

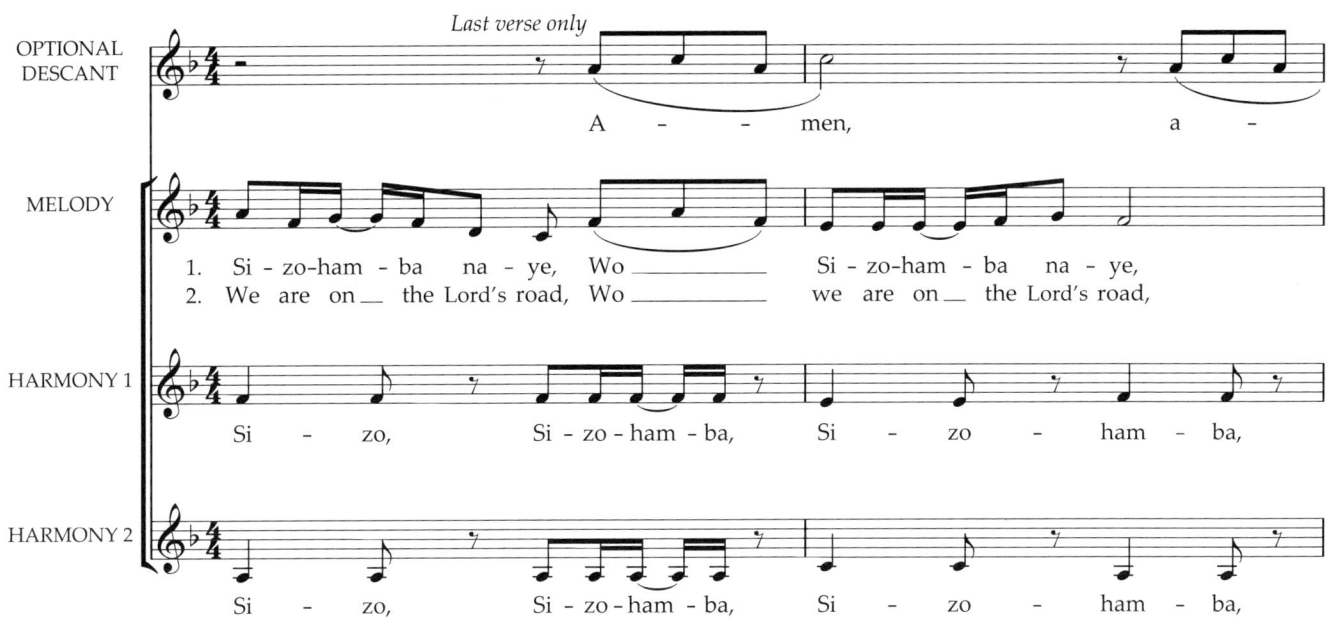

2. We are on the Lord's road, (Wo), We are on the Lord's road (x2)
   On our way to heaven we are on the Lord's road. (x2)

3. We shall sing the Lord's praise, (Wo), We shall sing the Lord's praise (x2)
   On our way to heaven we shall sing the Lord's praise. (x2)

4. We shall live the Lord's word, (Wo), We shall live the Lord's word (x2)
   On our way to heaven we shall live the Lord's word. (x2)

5. Hallelujah, Amen, (Wo), Hallelujah, Amen. (x2)
   Hallelujah, Amen. Hallelujah, Amen. (x2)

YOU MAY PHOTOCOPY THIS PAGE